DORLING KINDERSLEY DK EYEWITNESS GUIDES

FLAG

Japanese naval ensign from World War II, with "rising sun" design

Bunting

Chinese flag, 19th century, with figure of winged tiger

British heraldic crest with flag

DK EYEWITNESS GUIDES

FLAG

Written by
WILLIAM CRAMPTON

Badges from
World War I, showing flags
of France, Great Britain, and Belgium

Dice from early
20th-century flag game

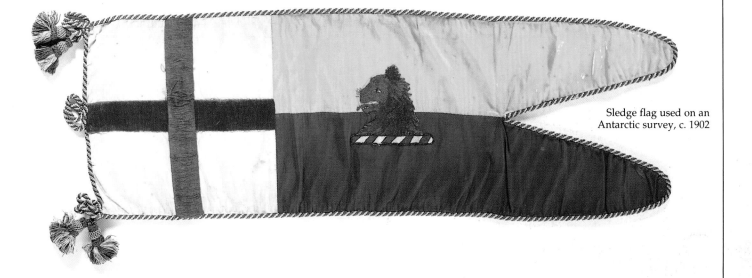

Sledge flag used on an
Antarctic survey, c. 1902

Dorling Kindersley

Chinese nationalist
flag of the 1920s

Olive branches,
common symbol of peace

Plastic marker flags
used in sports events

British heraldic shield

Dorling Kindersley

LONDON, NEW YORK, DELHI, JOHANNESBURG, MUNICH,
PARIS and SYDNEY

For a full catalogue, visit

DK www.dk.com

Project editor Phil Wilkinson
Art editor Peter Bailey
Senior editor Sophie Mitchell
Senior art editor Julia Harris
Managing art editor Roger Priddy
Managing editor Sue Unstead
Consultant Jos Poels

This Eyewitness ® Guide has been conceived by
Dorling Kindersley Limited and Editions Gallimard

First published in 1989
by Dorling Kindersley Limited
9 Henrietta Street, London WC2E 8PS

6 8 10 9 7

Seal of King Edward VII

Badge showing flag
of Spain

Stamp with flag of the
Chinese Liberation Army

Flag flown over headquarters
of a commando unit during
World War II

British Library Cataloguing in Publication data
Crampton, W.G. (William G.)
Flag
1. Flags
I. Title II. Series
929.9′2

ISBN 0-86318-370-0

Flag of Gazelle Force,
a British unit in the Sudan, 1940

Colour reproduction by Colourscan, Singapore
Printed in China by Toppan Printing Co. (Shenzhen) Ltd.

Army car pennant

Contents

Selection of flag badges

France, Britain, and Belgium

Canada, Britain, Australia, USA, New Zealand

Soviet flags

Palestine

Salvation Army

The anatomy of a flag

Flags come in all shapes and sizes. Usually they consist of a piece of free-flying fabric attached to a rigid vertical staff, although they may also be hung from horizontal bars. Flags may be flown from flag-poles or the halyards of sailing ships, carried on staves or spears, fixed on pins for table stands, or hung from spars at 45 degrees to the vertical known as "gaffs". Most modern flags are made from polyester, but many different fabrics have been used in the past, including silk, taffeta, cotton, linen, and wool. The designs may be built up by sewing together material of different colours, or they may be printed. In the past, elaborate designs were often painted or embroidered on to the surface of the flag and these methods are occasionally used today. Since the Renaissance most of the flags used at sea have been rectangular, and this is now the standard form for use on land, but military flags are traditionally square. Some flags flown by yachts are swallow-tailed or triangular, and heraldic banners are squarish.

British flag makers producing flags in the early 1950s.

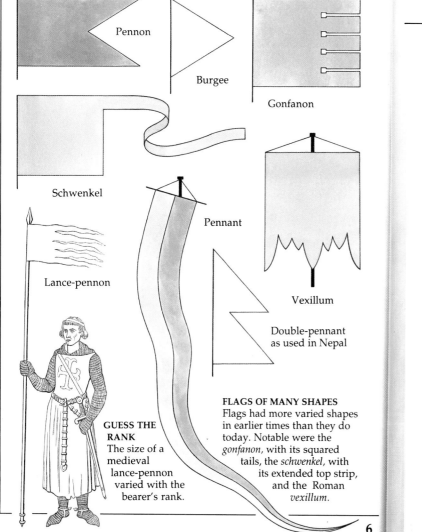

Pennon

Burgee

Gonfanon

Schwenkel

Pennant

Lance-pennon

Vexillum

Double-pennant as used in Nepal

GUESS THE RANK
The size of a medieval lance-pennon varied with the bearer's rank.

FLAGS OF MANY SHAPES
Flags had more varied shapes in earlier times than they do today. Notable were the *gonfanon*, with its squared tails, the *schwenkel*, with its extended top strip, and the Roman *vexillum*.

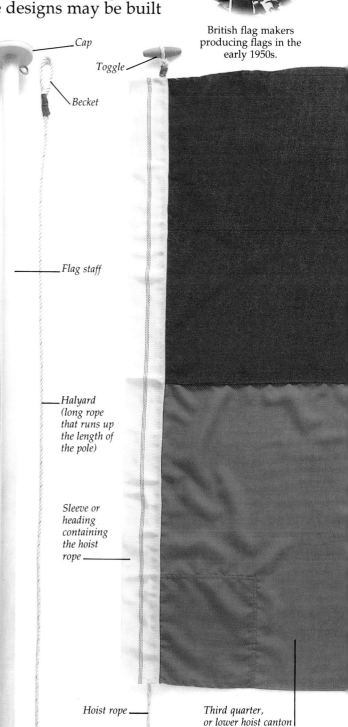

Cap

Toggle

Becket

Flag staff

Halyard (long rope that runs up the length of the pole)

Sleeve or heading containing the hoist rope

Hoist rope

Third quarter, or lower hoist canton

THE MONGOL CONQUEROR
This is a traditional view of the banner of the Mongol leader Ghengis Khan, with a flag of nine "feet" beneath four horse-tails. Chinese flags also had elaborately decorated ragged edges and coloured borders, but rarely contained emblems such as the hawk of the Mongols.

Second quarter, or upper fly canton

THE PARTS OF A FLAG
Flags are divided into four quarters, or *cantons*. The two nearest the pole form the *hoist* and the other two the *fly*. The upper canton of the hoist, which often contains a badge or emblem, is also often known simply as the *canton*. Flags for flying from a pole have a hollow tube of cloth called a *sleeve* or *heading* on the hoist side. Those made in Europe usually have a *hoist rope* sewn into this; American flags have an eyelet at either end. For indoor or parade use the flag staff is passed through the heading, and ropes and tassels are often attached to the decorative *finial* at the end of the pole. The horizontal dimension of a flag is the *length* and the vertical one the *width*.

MILITARY DECORATIONS
French military flags follow set patterns and are decorated with gold fringes and cravats (decorative streamers) attached just beneath the finial of the flag-staff. These carry honours awarded to the unit, and also its number in the line.

FOLDING THE FLAG
Military flags are hoisted, lowered, folded and stowed away according to set rules and rituals.

First quarter, or canton of the flag

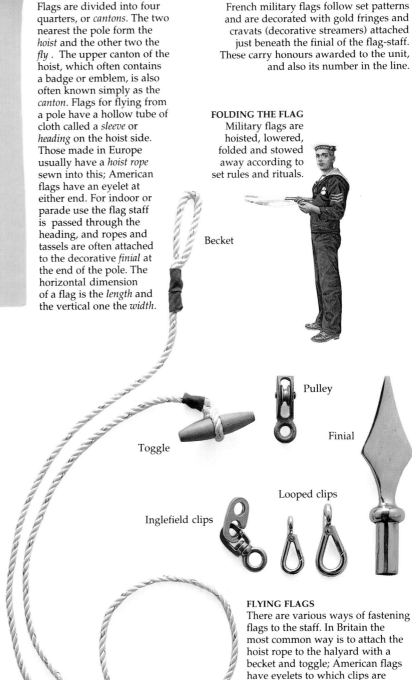

Becket

Toggle

Pulley

Finial

Looped clips

Inglefield clips

Fourth quarter, or lower fly canton

FLYING FLAGS
There are various ways of fastening flags to the staff. In Britain the most common way is to attach the hoist rope to the halyard with a becket and toggle; American flags have eyelets to which clips are attached. Inglefield clips (with their quick-release mechanism) are often used at sea. Indoor and parade flag staffs have elaborate finials.

First signs

EVIDENCE FROM EGYPT
This ancient Egyptian pot comes from the predynastic period (before 3000 BC). The object at the end of a pole on the right-hand side of the pot is a very early depiction of a flag-like object called a vexilloid.

WE USUALLY THINK OF A FLAG as a piece of fabric attached to a pole. But before flags as we know them were invented people carried poles topped with carved symbols. They used these objects in the same way that we use flags - to show loyalty to a leader or country, or to send signals. The first evidence for these solid flag-like objects comes from ancient Egypt, where they were used to distinguish various parts of the kingdom. The ancient civilizations of Greece, Rome, and the Middle East used them in similar ways. It was the ancient Romans who made most use of these symbols. Each unit of their army had its own standard, including the famous eagles of the legions. They also introduced the first true flag in the western world - the *vexillum*. This did not look like a modern flag because it was attached to a horizontal pole. Flags attached along one side to an upright pole first appeared in China, and were introduced to the west by the Arabs. But even then, flags were usually only made of plain fabric. Flags with actual designs on them became widespread during the Crusades. The Christians used the symbol of the cross, while the Moslems carried flags bearing inscriptions. In America, the Mexicans had developed flags made of feathers and the Aztecs had flags that could be carried on a warrior's back.

HOME-MADE FLAG
The first flag was probably no more than a piece of cloth tied to a stick, but it could still be used to attract attention or to send a message. Natural dyes could produce quite bright colours, like this red flag. A plain red flag still means danger today, just as it did in prehistoric times.

FLAG OR FAN?
The ancient Egyptians had vexilloids that could be carried or fixed on chariots. Some looked like fans; others consisted of carvings attached to poles.

BULL OF THE ASSYRIANS
The ancient Assyrians were a people who had a large empire in the Middle East. They were involved in many military campaigns, and had standards bearing figures of an archer on a bull's back and of two bulls. The standards were usually carried by charioteers.

ROMAN STANDARDS
The standards carried by Roman military units varied in design but all bore medals and badges. These two examples incorporate a vexillum (see below), which would have been a special award, and a hand, to ward off the evil eye. Other badges used by the Romans included portraits of the emperor, laurel wreaths, and crowns.

STREET IN CHINA
Chinese flags took a variety of forms, including ones like fans and streamers. Most relied on colour for their effect, rather than elaborate designs.

Finial on top of pole could contain legion badge

Painted figure

Silver ornaments

PRIDE OF A LEGION
This is a modern reconstruction of the Roman vexillum, the first true flag. It was the flag of a particular part of a legion, and was designed to be carried on horseback. The flag was a square of dark red cloth and the original could have had a picture or an inscription on it.

Name of legion

LE II AVG

Coats of arms

The basis of a coat of arms is the shield. This one is from a ceiling boss in a medieval building.

HERALDRY IS THE ART of producing and recording coats of arms. It has had a great influence on flags, creating new kinds of flags, and laying down ground rules for their design and use. Anyone who has a coat of arms can also use heraldic flags. Traditionally these are the long *standard*, the rectangular *banner*, the *badge-flag*, and the *pennon*. A coat of arms consists of the following items: a shield, which can contain symbols relevant to the history or background of the bearer's family; *supporters* on either side of the shield; and a helmet with a wreath, mantling, and a *crest* on top of the shield. There may also be a scroll and a motto. Arms, and the flags that go with them, are granted to one person only, and may not be used by anyone else.

STAMP OF APPROVAL
Personal heraldry - and heraldry of towns and cities - can be displayed on seals. Sometimes the whole coat of arms is shown; alternatively there can be an image of the bearer of the arms in full heraldic armour.

Wreath or "torse" in the "livery colours"of the arms

Crest always stands on top of wreath or "torse"

STANDARDS
Heraldic standards show the colours, arms badges and mottoes of the bearer. The relevant shields are shown alongside.

FOR DISPLAY
This helmet is not designed to be worn - it comes from a coat of arms and bears a wreath and crest. The double-headed eagle of the crest also bears a cross, as does the highly decorated helmet.

Helmet of the kind used in medieval tournaments

KNIGHTS OF OLD
Tournaments were great occasions for displays of heraldry, and usually included an exhibition of the armour, coats of arms and banners of those taking part.

ROYAL ARMS
At the time of Henry VIII the British royal coat of arms had the lion of England and the Red Dragon of Wales (one of the badges of the Tudor dynasty) as "supporters".

Churchill arms

Cadency mark to indicate a second son

Spencer arms

FOR A NATIONAL HERO
In Sir Winston Churchill's heraldic banner the background is the same as the shield of the coat of arms and the border of black and white is in the main colours of the arms. The arms incorporate those of Churchill's two lines of descent, the families of Churchill and Spencer.

Cloves

Tree peony

EASTERN SYMBOLS
Japanese heraldry uses highly stylized family badges known as *mon*. These can be borne on flags, used for decoration, or included on fans and clothing. Unlike European heraldic devices they do not have specific colours.

KNIGHT IN ARMOUR
Sir John Cornwall was an English knight of the 15th century. He is depicted with his coat of arms, heraldic standard, and a surcoat bearing his crest. The soldier behind him is carrying a standard bearing the arms of a member of the royal family of the period.

Royal standard

Surcoat

Standard of Sir John Cornwall

Shield

Wreath

Churchill's crest is a lion bearing a flag. It is quite unusual for heraldic crests to incorporate flags in this way. The heraldic term for the pose in which the lion is shown is *sejant* (or seated) with one paw raised.

Friend or foe?

In the confusion of the battlefield, flags provide an easy method of distinguishing friends from enemies. Flags were once a common sight wherever battle raged, and even today they are used by the military, both on land and at sea. In medieval times they identified individuals as well as groups, in the way that car flags and flags that fly over battlefield headquarters still do today. When armies became more organized (from the sixteenth century onwards), their individual regiments and companies developed their own flags. These were known as Colours, and they were often elaborately decorated with embroidered coats of arms. Colours eventually became more important for ceremonies - more durable flags are now used in battle.

COMING OF THE CONQUEROR
The Norman knights at the Battle of Hastings in 1066 carried small flags called *pennons* on their lances. Duke William had an elaborate one sent to him by the Pope. This and other flags were illustrated in the Bayeux Tapestry.

WHO WAS WHO?
Medieval knights could easily be identified because they carried their personal emblems on their shields and banners.

Initials of the Ringwood Light Dragoons

Royal cypher of King George III

THE CAVALRY ARE COMING
A descendant of the medieval lance-pennon is the cavalry guidon. This one dates from the Napoleonic Wars and was meant to be carried on horseback.

Royal badge of the White Horse of Hanover

Lancer with pennon attached to his lance

Sleeve could be nailed to the lance

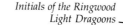

Very deep swallow-tail

BADGE OF THE BRITISH
The lance-pennons of the British army are always red over white and swallow-tailed. This one is from a troop of Indian lancers.

LANCERS
Lances were still used even in the days of firearms. A famous example was the ill-fated Charge of the Light Brigade in the Crimean War, during which many British lancers met their death.

THE SWASTIKA

The Nazi swastika was one of the best-known party symbols of modern times. Originally a sun-symbol, it was used in many different ways before it became the national flag of Germany in 1935. This version was used as a wall-hanging. The swastika flag was replaced in 1945 (pp. 28-9).

PACIFIC OVERTURES
This World War II poster represents American victories over the Japanese.

Union Jack

Square shape indicates use as wall-hanging

PROPAGANDA FLAG
This flag, made during World War I, shows the German national flag of the period beneath the Union Jack. The motto *Deutschland unter Alles* ("Germany under all") is a parody of a phrase from the German national anthem.

DEUTSCHLAND UNTER ALLES

German flag

SIDE BY SIDE
The United States, France, Britain, and Italy are among the World War I allies shown here. The flagstaffs are topped by decorative finials, a common feature of military flags.

LIBERTÉ EGALITE FRATERNITE

UN SEUL COMBAT POUR UNE SEULE PATRIE

ONE WAR
The slogan on this poster from World War II means "One struggle for one country".

The flags of Britain, France, and Belgium

UNITED WE STAND

The arms and flag of Belgium

Japan (the Rising Sun)

Russia (the Naval Ensign)

France

Britain

FLAGS FOR ALL
Devices showing the united flags of the Allies were very common during World War II. They took a variety of forms, including badges, handkerchiefs, scarves, cards, and games.

Belgium

FLAG GAME
This game consists of dice with an allied flag on each face.

FRIEND IN NEED
Flags can still be used for identification in modern warfare. They are especially useful because they are international symbols that anyone can understand. This piece of cloth was designed to be carried by British airmen serving in Eastern Europe during World War II. It bears the message "I am British", and an instruction to contact the local British Military Mission.

Я англичанин

" Ya Anglicháhnin " *(Pronounced as spelt)*

Пожалуйста сообщите сведения обо мне в Британскую Военную Миссию в Москве

Please communicate my particulars to British Military Mission Moscow

13

Showing your colours

FLYING HOME
The house flag of the Scottish shipping line of MacCann bears the classical emblem of Pegasus, the winged horse, to represent speed.

MANY FLAGS INCLUDE SYMBOLS that are used to express ideas which would otherwise take many words. These symbols derive from many different sources – from animals to plants, weapons to everyday objects. One of the best-known examples is the lion in medieval heraldry, which represented both kingship and bravery. Colours are also given symbolic meanings. We use white and blue to represent peace in flags like that of the United Nations. And green is the colour of vegetation, but has also been used to represent youth and hope. Religious ideas are among the oldest to be expressed in flag form and the cross is the oldest device in heraldry. In Moslem countries the crescent moon has been a symbol of religion since at least the 14th century, although the crescent combined with a star is not so old. Another Islamic symbol is the double-bladed sword, which represents the Prophet's son-in-law, Ali. Islamic law does not allow the depiction of God or people, but other countries have no such restrictions and there are many Chinese flags that depict gods and Christian flags that show images of saints. Modern symbols include the Canadian maple leaf and the hammer and sickle of the former Soviet Union.

Hammer and sickle

WORKERS UNITE!
The tools of the industrial and the agricultural labourer (the "Workers" and "Peasants" of the Russian Revolution) appeared in stylized form on the flag of the former Soviet Uni

Flag of former USSR

HOLY WAR?
In this illustration of tribal warfare in 19th century Morocco, the green Islamic flag is prominent.

WELLINGTON'S CREST
The combination of the king of beasts with the flag of victory rising from a ducal coronet forms an appropriate crest for the Duke of Wellington.

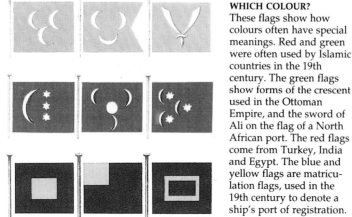

WHICH COLOUR?
These flags show how colours often have special meanings. Red and green were often used by Islamic countries in the 19th century. The green flags show forms of the crescent used in the Ottoman Empire, and the sword of Ali on the flag of a North African port. The red flags come from Turkey, India and Egypt. The blue and yellow flags are matriculation flags, used in the 19th century to denote a ship's port of registration.

Flag of Canada

Red maple leaf

CANADIAN MAPLE
For ease of manufacture and reproduction on the flag of Canada the red maple leaf has been reduced to a highly stylized form, making a new heraldic emblem. This has happened to all the devices used in flags and coats of arms.

FLOWER OF POWER
Japanese heraldry stylizes objects more even than European heraldry, to produce symbolic designs called *mon*. Here the chrysanthemum on the Emperor's standard bears little resemblance to the actual flower.

Chrysanthemum

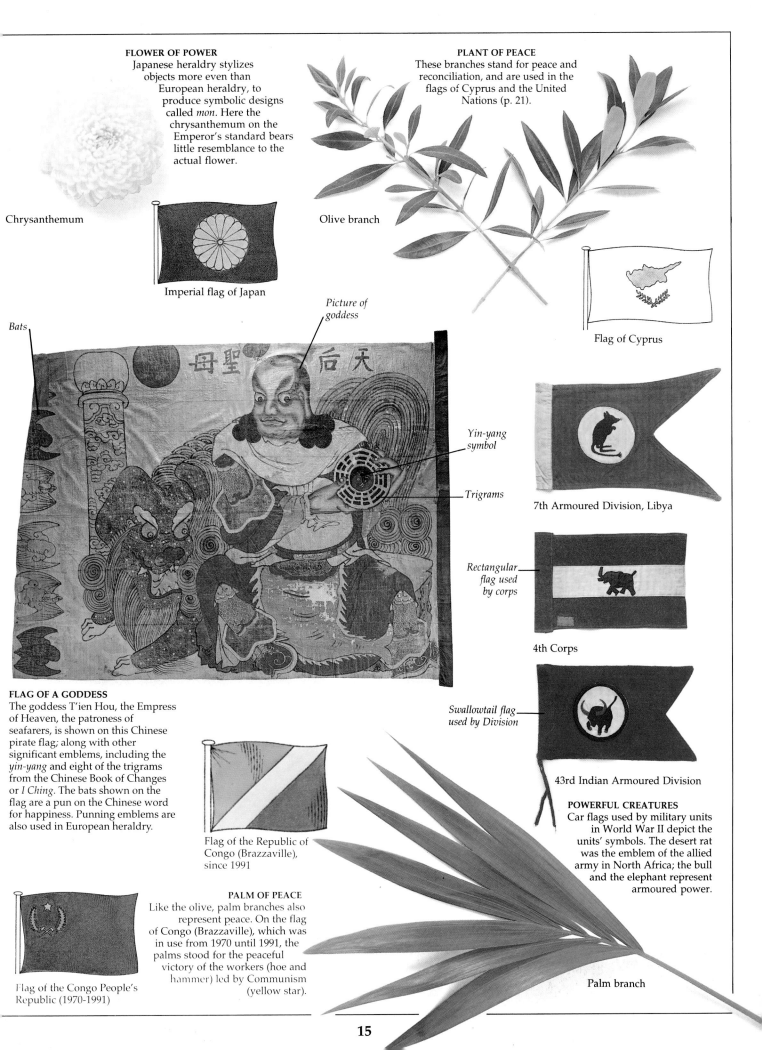

Imperial flag of Japan

PLANT OF PEACE
These branches stand for peace and reconciliation, and are used in the flags of Cyprus and the United Nations (p. 21).

Olive branch

Flag of Cyprus

Picture of goddess

Bats

Yin-yang symbol

Trigrams

7th Armoured Division, Libya

Rectangular flag used by corps

4th Corps

Swallowtail flag used by Division

43rd Indian Armoured Division

FLAG OF A GODDESS
The goddess T'ien Hou, the Empress of Heaven, the patroness of seafarers, is shown on this Chinese pirate flag; along with other significant emblems, including the *yin-yang* and eight of the trigrams from the Chinese Book of Changes or *I Ching*. The bats shown on the flag are a pun on the Chinese word for happiness. Punning emblems are also used in European heraldry.

Flag of the Republic of Congo (Brazzaville), since 1991

POWERFUL CREATURES
Car flags used by military units in World War II depict the units' symbols. The desert rat was the emblem of the allied army in North Africa; the bull and the elephant represent armoured power.

PALM OF PEACE
Like the olive, palm branches also represent peace. On the flag of Congo (Brazzaville), which was in use from 1970 until 1991, the palms stood for the peaceful victory of the workers (hoe and hammer) led by Communism (yellow star).

Flag of the Congo People's Republic (1970-1991)

Palm branch

Setting sail

DRESSED OVERALL
On occasions such as holidays or celebrations of important victories, ships used to fly all their available flags, producing an effect like this. Today only signal flags are used to "dress ship".

Sɪɴᴄᴇ ᴛʜᴇ ᴅᴀʏꜱ ᴏꜰ ᴛʜᴇ ꜰɪʀꜱᴛ ᴡᴀʀꜱʜɪᴘꜱ and the earliest trading vessels, flags have always been used at sea. Today such ships - as well as the thousands of passenger ships and the boats of all shapes and sizes that are used for recreation - still use flags. All ships over a certain size are supposed to display their national colours, although many do not do so. In practice this means that they should fly their national or mercantile flag or naval ensign. For American ships, for example, the Stars and Stripes plays all these roles, whereas British ships fly one of the three British Ensigns. About twenty other nations are like Britain in having separate national and mercantile flags, and one or two have separate national flags for yachts. In addition, commercial shipping lines display their individual house flags. Other flag traditions include flying the relevant national flag when entering a foreign port - this is known as flying a "courtesy flag". On leaving port, many ships fly the blue flag with a white square in the centre called the Blue Peter.

Material is orange damask silk

Yin-yang symbol representing the coming together of opposites

Trigrams from the I Ching

PHILOSOPHICAL FLAG
This pennant comes from a Chinese junk. It illustrates some of the key ideas in traditional Chinese thought, with the yin-yang symbol at the hoist and the eight trigrams from the Book of Changes or *I Ching* prominently displayed along the length of the flag. The pennant also has a ragged edge, typical of Chinese flags.

BRITISH ENSIGNS
The White Ensign is the form of the British national flag used exclusively on ships of the Royal Navy. The Red and Blue Ensigns are also British national flags for use at sea - the first for civilian vessels and the second for ships on government service.

TUDOR FLAGSHIP
The flagship of Henry VIII's navy, the *Henry Grace à Dieu*, was decorated with the flags of England and flags representing the House of Tudor. The royal livery colours were green and white during this period.

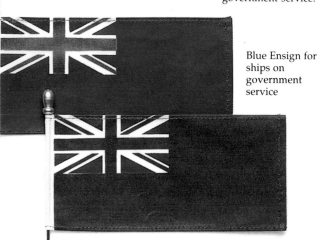

Blue Ensign for ships on government service

Red Ensign for civil vessels

Toggle

Lion and crown from
East India Company's arms

EAST INDIA COMPANY
The broad pennant of Sir Robert Oliver, commander of the Indian Navy in the days of the British East India Company, a trading company that eventually took over the government of much of India. The flag has a striking shape with tails of different lengths. The lion holding a crown is from the crest of the Company's arms. The flag was in use from 1848-63, when the navy was transferred to the British Crown. The red part of the flag is made of woollen fabric, but the lion and cross are silk.

Extra piece
of material to
make repair

Hoist rope

FROM THE CHINA SEAS
This flag from a Chinese junk has a shape and design that is typical of the flags of the China Sea in the last century. The main motif is a dragon, and the inscriptions can be translated as "Lord of Suiyan" and "Spirit Banner".

BALL ON SHIPBOARD
In Tissot's famous painting of a ball on board ship (c. 1874) the deck is canopied with the contents of the ship's flag locker. The display includes several royal standards and national flags, but using them in this way would be considered disrespectful today.

Typical ragged
(or "invected")
border, with
lightning flashes

Material is silk
damask with
gold appliqué

BATTLE COLOURS
The Austrian and Italian fleets engage at the Battle of Lissa (1866). National and signalling flags, together with long pennants, can be seen.

Hollow linen sleeve for mounting on bamboo pole

Signalling with flags

SIGNALLING AT SEA is one of the oldest uses of flags. Signals were made with flag-like objects called "vexilloids" (see pp. 8-9) on both sides in the wars between the Greeks and Persians (547-478 BC), but by the Middle Ages the Genoese and Venetian fleets had more elaborate signals. The first specially made signal flag was the "Banner of the Council" introduced for the English fleet in 1369 (used to summon captains to the Admiral's ship). Otherwise signals were made by hoisting ordinary flags in special positions. The first regular code of flag signals dates from the seventeenth century in England and in the following century numeral flags were invented, which could be combined to make up messages. Each ship also had pennants to represent its name, and the numbers could also represent letters of the alphabet. In 1812 Sir Home Popham introduced special flags for letters of the alphabet and by 1889 there was a flag for each letter and numeral. The first International Code of Signals was introduced on 1 January 1900. Flag signalling, with semaphore and other flags, also exists on land.

COURTESY FLAG
A ship about to enter a foreign port hoists the flag of that country as a courtesy (p. 16).

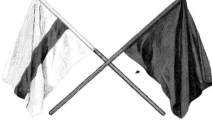

Pair of semaphore flags

ALL ABOARD
Railways used many flag signals before the advent of electronic signalling. These examples are signals to the engine driver from the platform.

CODE OF SIGNALS
This is flag 19, the letter O (Oscar), from the International Code of Signals. As well as representing the letters of the alphabet, the flags also indicate a particular message. This one represents the signal "Man overboard". Signal flags are usually made in proportions of 5:6.

MORSE CODE
During the American Civil War, a signalling method was developed that used a single flag to represent the dots and dashes of the Morse Code.

SEMAPHORE
The semaphore system of signalling involves changing the positions of both arms to represent different letters and numbers. This is the semaphore signal for the letter C.

The letter E in the flag semaphore code.

WARNING SIGN
In the 19th century, flags were sometimes attached to buoys at sea. They made the buoy more easily visible as well as giving important information.

CALL TO PRAYER
The Church Pennant, the signal that a religious service is about to take place on board ship, is used in the British Navy. It combines the flags of England and Holland, and dates from the 17th century.

Inglefield clip

TRAFALGAR
Nelson's flagship, HMS Victory, is seen here with another British ship, HMS Temeraire at the Battle of Trafalgar in 1805. Nelson was skilful in his use in his use of signals to manoeuvre his ships into the correct positions for battle.

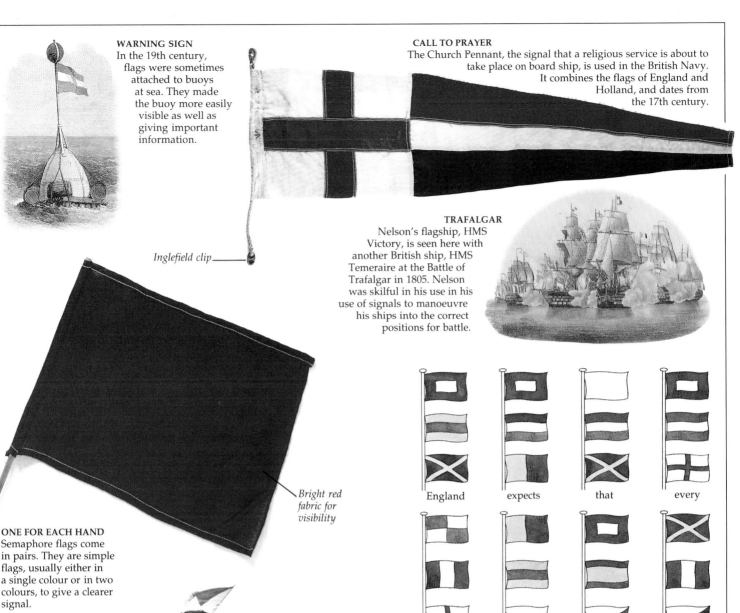

Bright red fabric for visibility

ONE FOR EACH HAND
Semaphore flags come in pairs. They are simple flags, usually either in a single colour or in two colours, to give a clearer signal.

England	expects	that	every
man	will	do	his
D	U	T	Y

SPECIAL OCCASION
This modern battleship has been decorated with an array of signal flags for a ceremonial occasion.

ENGLAND EXPECTS...
Nelson's famous signal at Trafalgar 1805 was composed of "hoists" taken from Sir Home Popham's *Dictionary of Signals*, except for the last word, "Duty". This did not appear in the dictionary, and had to be spelled out using the numerals from the official signal book of 1803. Nelson also wanted to use the word "confides", but this was also absent from the dictionary.

The letter X in the semaphore system.

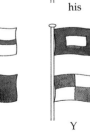

The "ready" position in the semaphore system

Flags of the people

MANY FLAGS START LIFE being locally designed and made by individuals in response to the need for symbols of religious, political, or social action. Such flag designers do not always pay attention to the strict rules of heraldry or of flag design, and so the flags they produce are usually spontaneous and simply made. They often include very simple symbols (such as the black crab from the Southern Cameroons shown opposite) and many also have some sort of inscription (whether a religious text or a political slogan). Some go on to become well-established political or national flags but others exist only for the moment. They are often subject to local changes and variations and are rarely made in a standard form. But this seldom matters to their users because, unlike national flags, they are more often used to rally the faithful than for identification.

LAMB AND FLAG
This was an enduring religious symbol in the Middle Ages.

FOR LIBERTY
The tricolour cockade is visible in this scene from the time of the French Revolution (pp. 26-27).

SWAPO flag

ANC flag

Early 20th-century Armenian flag

FLAGS OF STRUGGLE
Nationalist movements often use badges of their emblems and colours. The flag of the African National Congress was banned in South Africa, but supporters still found ways of displaying the colours. Armenia chose a new flag after independence (p. 57). The SWAPO flag formed the basis of independent Namibia's flag (p. 62).

SOLIDARITY
This symbol incorporates both flag and people.

Rainbow symbol represents Greenpeace

FLAG OF THE "GREENS"
This is one form of the flag of Greenpeace, the international movement for protecting the earth's environment. The emblems of the dove, the olive branch, and the rainbow are all taken from the Biblical story of the flood. The green background symbolizes the conservation of the environment and is also a symbol of hope.

Green for the environment and hope

DAY OF THE LORD
Roman Catholic festivals and processions often feature large religious banners. These examples are painted with subjects such as the Virgin and Child.

THE RED FLAG
These Chinese demonstrators are carrying red flags, international symbols of socialism.

FLAG OF RESISTANCE
The *Union des Populations du Cameroun* was a resistance movement in the Cameroons in the 1960s, which now exists only in exile. This example of their flag was captured by British troops before the Southern Cameroons joined the Cameroon Republic.

DERVISH FLAG
This flag from the Sudan was taken by the British in 1885. It contains an inscription from the Koran, and is said to have belonged to the Moslem leader called the Mahdi.

LENIN
Many propaganda posters from the Soviet Union included the red flag.

FLAG OF HEALING
The white background of the Red Cross flag represents peace, and the cross is inspired by the cross of Switzerland (p. 33). A red crescent is used in Moslem countries.

UNITING THE NATIONS
The blue of the United Nations flag is a distinctive pale shade, now known as "United Nations Blue". The olive branches stand for peace and reconciliation.

CHURCH BANNER
The Omega Workshop designed and produced many fine textiles in the 1920s, including this banner.

Flags for sport and celebration

Flags ARE USED IN MANY SPORTS, including all water sports, motor-racing, team games, golf, gymnastics, skiing, and cross-country events. They are employed as signals, markers, team signs, supporters' favours, and decorations. They also signal the opening and closing of the events. Each Olympic Games has its own flag, and the well-known flag of the Olympic movement itself dates from 1914 and has five coloured rings that represent the five continents. When medals are presented to the victors in the Games their national anthems are played, and the opening and closing of the Games is signalled by the hoisting and lowering of the Olympic Standard.

WEAVING THEIR WAY THROUGH
Flags are used as markers in many skiing events, but in slalom they define the exact path the competitor has to follow.

Sports fans encourage their heroes with flags and use them to show which side they are supporting - here Liverpool and Everton.

LINESMEN'S FLAGS
Soccer linesmen use flags to signal to the referee when the ball has gone out of play or when players have broken the rules of the game. Flags are also used in soccer to mark the corners of the playing area.

Swivel fitting for greater flexibility

One flag in each team colour

Wooden handle

Cork handle

AID TO EXERCISE
In rhythmic gymnastics, the competitors perform exercises with long streamers that are meant to be light, bright, conspicuous, and graceful.

Russian rhythmic gymnast
Galina Krilenko

22

MARKERS

Small plastic flags in a range of colours are used in many sports as markers. They are sometimes employed in cricket to mark the boundary line, and often used to mark the course in cross-country running.

Point sticks in ground

RUNNER UP *below*

The flag is waved ceremoniously as the winner passes the line, but the end of the race is signalled to the runners up by holding the flag still.

SIGN OF VICTORY

The best-known flag in motor-racing is the Chequered Flag, used to designate the winner and to close the race. The race is always started with the local national flag, and many other flags are used as signals to the drivers.

Can be made of any material, including PVC

Tape joining flags together

PUT OUT MORE FLAGS

Bunting - strings of miniature flags which can be triangular or rectangular - is a common form of decoration at sports events and other occasions. Bunting comes in team colours, national colours, or neutral shades, and may even carry logos and advertisements. It provides a traditional and colourful way of decorating buildings, and can be strung from pole to pole at any outdoor event.

OLYMPIC FLAG

The Olympic symbol of five interlinked rings is used in many different ways on the flags of the participating countries. Special flags like this are sometimes used when a team takes part in the Games but does not represent its country officially.

Streamer made of ribbon

The United States of America

WHO WAS THE FIRST?
Robert Peary was the first man to reach the North Pole. He asserted his claim by hoisting the Stars and Stripes. His claim was disputed by Frederick Cook.

THE STARS AND STRIPES is the best-known flag in the world, but little is known for sure about its origin. It was not designed by one person but evolved gradually. Its first form was the Cambridge (or "Grand Union") Flag of the winter of 1775-6, which had thirteen stripes and the British Union Flag in the canton. In 1777 it was decided to replace the Union Flag with the blue canton and 13 stars. It is not certain exactly how the stars were first arranged - the law of 1777 refers simply to the 13 stars representing "a new constellation" - and many different designs were made. There is a legend that Betsy Ross of Philadelphia made the first flag and presented it to George Washington, but it is more likely that Francis Hopkinson (the creator of the seal of the USA) had a hand in the design. After independence it was thought that each star and each stripe represented a state, although it was later decided to increase only the number of stars when a new state joined the union.

SURRENDER OF CORNWALLIS
This famous painting shows the flags of the USA and of France (the Americans' ally), as they were supposed to be in 1781.

CAMBRIDGE FLAG
Adopted for Washington's Continental army, this flag was also called the "Continental Colors".

FIRST STARS AND STRIPES
This is the most familiar version of the first Stars and Stripes, although its exact form is uncertain.

FLAG OF THE SOUTH
This flag was used in a square form in the American Civil War. The modern form is shown here.

SOUTHERN STATE
The flag of the state of Mississippi has the Southern battle flag in the canton. It was adopted after the American Civil War.

STARS AND BARS
This was the first flag of the Confederacy of Southern States that broke away at the start of the Civil War. It flew over Fort Sumpter, South Carolina, after the first shots in the war were fired there on 12 April 1861.

AMERICAN LEGION FLAG
This is the flag of a force raised from American citizens living in Canada during World War I. The flag was presented to the Legion by American-born ladies of Canada and is decorated with gold fringes and tassles.

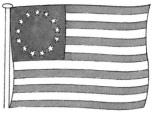

STATE FLAGS
Each American state has its own flag, as well as a coat of arms or seal. This example, from Illinois, is being waved at a Republican Convention at Dallas. The central device is derived from the state seal.

50 stars - one for each of today's states

13 stripes for the original 13 states

The specifications for the construction of the flag were laid down in 1912 and those for the colours were written in 1934. The flag is in proportions of 10:19. Alterations in the layout and number of the stars are made on the orders of the President. There are national and local laws to protect the flag from abuse.

THE STARS AND STRIPES

After independence it was thought that each star and stripe represented one state, and that their number had to be increased as the union expanded. But in 1818 it was decided to increase the number of stars only, and to keep the thirteen stripes. The present form of the Stars and Stripes dates from 4 July 1960, when a fiftieth star was added for Hawaii. Alterations to the flag take place on 4 July following the admission of a new state, and there have been 26 changes since 1777. Particular stars do not represent named states - it is simply the total that corresponds to the number of states in the Union.

GOOD CAUSES

The tricolour, used by Afro-Americans, is sometimes called the Black Liberation Flag. The Christian flag, created in 1897 by Charles Overton, represents Christians of all denominations.

SYMBOL OF A NATION *above*

The flag can be used for anything from promoting war bonds to advertising ice-cream. But however it is used, it is above all a patriotic symbol for Americans all over the world. "Uncle Sam" is the personification of America, and is always shown dressed in the Stars and Stripes.

IWO JIMA

The famous photograph of marines raising the US flag on Iwo Jima (during the Pacific War in World War II) has been transformed into their national memorial, an unusual instance of a real flag being combined with a piece of sculpture. The raising of the flag on Iwo Jima is a powerful symbol of the part played by the USA - and the American flag - in World War II.

FLAG ON THE MOON

One of the functions of the national flag is to symbolize conquest - including scientific and peaceful conquest.

France

SOME OF THE MOST WELL-KNOWN flags in history come from France. The first was the *Oriflamme,* used up to the time of the French defeat at the battle of Agincourt in 1451 and recognizable because of its unusual, many-tailed shape (p. 6). Second were the many flags that used the traditional emblem of France, the lily. Just before the revolution in 1789 the national flag was plain white, the colour of the reigning Bourbon kings, although command flags were still decorated with lilies. The royal standard was white with gold lilies all over it, surmounted by the royal arms. But the most famous French flag of all is the red, white, and blue flag called the *Tricolore,* used during the revolution in 1789, and familiar as a symbol of liberty throughout the world. Its colours were adopted by naval ships in 1790, although the red stripe was placed at the hoist. The *Tricolore* as we know it today was introduced in 1794, and, apart from a short time in the nineteenth century, has been in use ever since.

TRIUMPHANT RETURN
Napoleon wore his three-coloured cockade in his hat when riding into Paris in 1815.

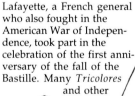

STANDARD BEARER
This Napoleonic soldier bears a *Tricolore,* topped with one of the eagles given to the regiments by the emperor.

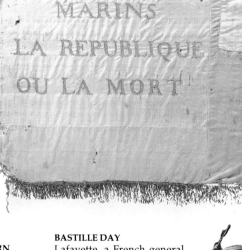

FOR REVOLUTION
This flag was made on board the French ship *L'Amerique* at the Battle of the First of June 1794. The inscription reads "Sailors, the Republic or death".

THE ROYAL LILY
The French king Charles V used the *fleur de lys* as his emblem. Here it decorates his robes, and his horse's coat, and his trumpeters' banners.

ROYAL RETURN
Between 1815 and 1830 the Bourbon kings of France returned to the throne. They used the simplified form of the royal arms shown on this standard.

BASTILLE DAY
Lafayette, a French general who also fought in the American War of Independence, took part in the celebration of the first anniversary of the fall of the Bastille. Many *Tricolores* and other banners can be seen.

THE *TRICOLORE*

The blue and red stripes of the *Tricolore* probably derive from the colours of Paris, while white is the colour of the Bourbon dynasty. The red, white, and blue flag has been the inspiration of many other flags that use these colours as symbols of liberty.

GIFT OF AN EMPEROR

Napoleon granted many colours with an eagle finial. This example was given to his Guard when he was in exile on the island of Elba. The bees were the emperor's personal emblem.

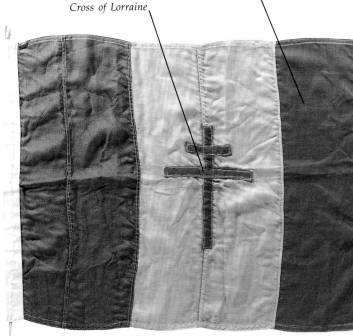

Cross of Lorraine

Unequal stripes show that flag was made for use at sea

FREE FRENCH FLAG

The jack of the Free French ships during the World War II bore the double-armed cross of Lorraine. This was the emblem of General Charles de Gaulle.

Germany

GERMAN EAGLE
Germany's traditional emblem, the black double-headed eagle, is seen here in a piece of stained-glass showing the arms of the city of Lübeck.

GERMANY IS A COUNTRY that is very rich in flags, with two distinct rival flag traditions based on two different colour combinations. Flags of both these traditions can be found in several forms. The oldest German colours are black, red, and gold, and their use on a flag dates from the time of the Napoleonic Wars - before Germany was a truly unified country. A black, red, and gold flag was adopted by the first all-German parliament at Frankfurt in 1848, but from 1867 to 1945 a black, white, and red flag was also used. The flag was designed by the Prussian Chancellor Bismarck, who unified the German states into a new Empire in 1871. In 1919 the black-red-gold flag was again adopted, but the black, white, and red colours were eventually re-imposed by Hitler in the form of the Swastika flag (p. 13). Like Bismarck, Hitler took a close interest in the German flag, and designed the Swastika flag himself. After the defeat of the Nazis both new German states returned to the black-red-gold.

LION
This lion is from a 15th-century coat of arms.

FOR THE NAVY
This flag, in use between 1903 and 1921, is the *Reichskriegsflagge* or Naval Ensign. Based on similar previous designs, the flag features the single-headed Prussian eagle in the centre. In the canton is the national flag with the Iron Cross, a Prussian emblem derived from the Teutonic Knights of the Middle Ages. The large black cross is inspired by the British White Ensign.

Iron Cross

Black and white colours of Prussia

Emblem of Frederick I of Prussia

Imperial crown

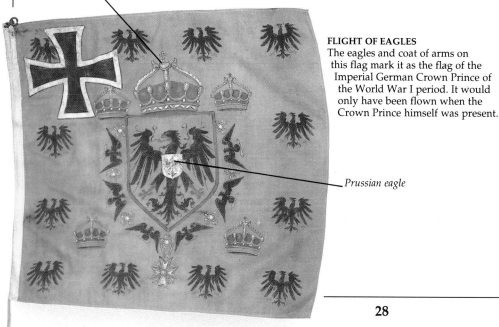

Prussian eagle

FLIGHT OF EAGLES
The eagles and coat of arms on this flag mark it as the flag of the Imperial German Crown Prince of the World War I period. It would only have been flown when the Crown Prince himself was present.

KISSING THE FLAG
A German soldier salutes his flag in this patriotic picture from World War I. Such images were often printed on postcards.

The black, red and gold tricolour is now the flag of a united Germany, following the reunification of 3 October 1990. Previously, the flags of the two parts of Germany were distinguished by the emblem placed on the East German version. The West German version with the shield of arms in the centre is only for government use. The shield is gold with a black single-headed eagle.

THE "BLACK-RED-GOLD"

The black, red, and gold tricolour was adopted again in West Germany on 8 May 1949. The colours derive from the uniform worn by troops of a regiment called the Lützow *Freikorps* in 1814, which was black and red with gold decorations; the flag was given the form of a tricolour a few years later. It was adopted at Frankfurt for the new united Germany of 1848. In 1919, it was re-adopted by the new German Republic, but abolished with the Nazi takeover in 1933. In 1948, it was restored in East Germany as a symbol of a re-formed country, and also subsequently in the West. Parallel versions were used in East and West Germany until 1990.

On flag arms appear in colour

Badge showing arms of East Germany

THE OPPOSITION *below*

The Communist *Roter Frontkämpfer Bund* (League of Red Front Campaigners) used red flags like this during the years they were in conflict with the Nazis.

THE GATHERING STORM

The Nazis were famous for their use of flags and banners on all occasions from political rallies to army marches. The swastika appeared on the standards of the Nazi SA (*Sturm Abteilung*) together with the spread eagle, and their motto *Deutschland erwache* ("Germany awake!").

Netherlands and Belgium

THE DUTCH TRICOLOUR was the first national flag in the modern sense of the word. It dates from the sixteenth century, when the Netherlands were ruled by Spain and the people were struggling against their Spanish overlords. At this time the upper stripe was orange, from the colours of William I, Prince of Orange. By 1630, however, it had changed to red, the colour of the Dutch States-General, although orange still plays an important part in Dutch national heraldry. The southern provinces (the area now covered by Belgium) had broken away by 1580, and remained dependencies until 1830. This was when the kingdom of Belgium was established and the present Belgian tricolour introduced. The rampant lion is common to both countries (it is yellow on black in Belgium, red on yellow in Holland). The orange-white-blue colours of the Netherlands have been adopted in several places originally colonized by the Dutch, including the city of New York.

WILLIAM OF ORANGE
The colours of the House of Orange were used in the first Dutch flags.

TROPHIES FROM SPAIN
The flags taken from the Spaniards by the Dutch were hung up in the Ridderzaal in the Hague (meeting place of the States-General). Most were naval flags, and bore the red cross of Burgundy.

Belgian tricolour

Lion of Brabant

BELGIAN ARMS
The gold lion on black represents Brabant, but also forms the national arms of Belgium, adopted after independence in 1830. The motto is that of the States-General ("Unity is Strength"). Around the crest are the banners of the provinces.

FLAG FOR LIBERTY
First Belgium (1792) and then the Netherlands (1795) were taken over by the French. The Netherlands became the Batavian Republic in 1796 and adopted the Dutch tricolour with a canton depicting the figure of Liberty holding the republican emblems (axes and rods, and the cap of liberty). This version was the flag used by Admiral de Winter at the Battle of Camperdown (1797).

CITY PRIDE
All Dutch cities and towns have their own flags. The lion of Holland can be seen on the flag of Zeeland, and water-lily leaves on the flag of Friesland.

Langedijk   Zeeland   Friesland

The Belgian flag being waved at a royal wedding

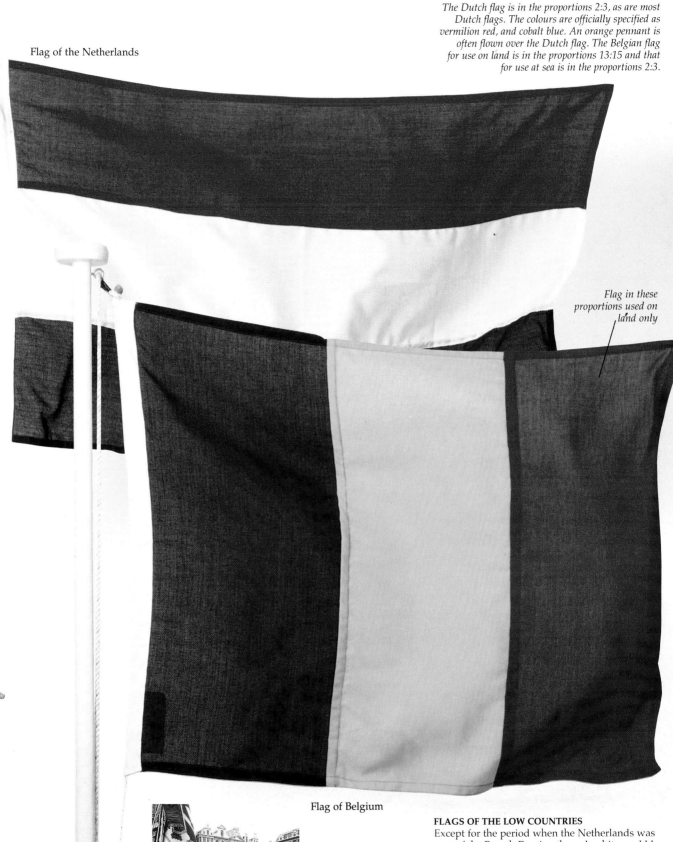

Flag of the Netherlands

*The Dutch flag is in the proportions 2:3, as are most
Dutch flags. The colours are officially specified as
vermilion red, and cobalt blue. An orange pennant is
often flown over the Dutch flag. The Belgian flag
for use on land is in the proportions 13:15 and that
for use at sea is in the proportions 2:3.*

*Flag in these
proportions used on
land only*

Flag of Belgium

BELGIAN PARADE
The Grand' Place in
Brussels often sees
flag ceremonies, as
in this one involving
visitors from the
Austrian Tyrol.

FLAGS OF THE LOW COUNTRIES
Except for the period when the Netherlands was
part of the French Empire, the red, white, and blue
tricolour has flown over the Dutch state since the
early seventeenth century. It was made official in
1937. The Belgian tricolour emerged from the
struggle against the Dutch in 1830, and was at first
made in horizontal form. The colours are those of
the arms of Brabant and the same colours are
found in the arms of the provinces. It has been
used in vertical form since January 1831.

Austria and Switzerland

THE ORIGINAL REGIONS (or "cantons") of Switzerland were ruled by Austrian Dukes until the fourteenth century, when they threw off Austrian rule and formed a loose confederation which was joined by other Swiss states. The emblem that they chose derives from the symbol of the central canton of Schwyz. It was adopted by the other cantons as a battle flag in 1339 and as a common banner in 1480, but it was not widely used as a national flag until after 1848. Austria, meanwhile, grew into a large empire, which lasted until 1918. The red and white colours of Austria are derived from the arms of the Dukes who were in power at the time of the struggle with Switzerland; their colours have been used in this form since at least 1230. Both Austria and Swtizerland have strong heraldic traditions along German lines (pp. 28-9) and every region has its own arms and flag. Many of the Swiss regional flags contain heraldic emblems, whereas the the majority of the Austrian flags are plainer striped designs.

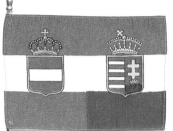

FLAG OF AN EMPIRE
From 1867 to 1918 Austria and Hungary were ruled by the same emperor. The Austro-Hungarian empire used this flag at sea, which combines both their colours and shields.

This figure carries a flag in the Imperial colours of Austria.

Bern

LOCAL BANNERS
Most cantons of Switzerland use their armorial banners as local flags. They have the same designs as their coats of arms. The flag of Bern has the image of a bear, which can be seen all over the city. The flag of Uri portrays a wild ox, after which the canton is named. That of Lucerne uses the same colours as the local arms, but these are arranged in horizontal bands rather than the vertical ones of the shield.

Lucerne

PROUD AND PROMINENT
There is a famous display of flags on the Pont de Mont Blanc, Geneva. Visible are those of the Swiss cantons Thurgau, Bern, Fribourg, Glarus, and Graubünden.

Uri

NATIONAL HERO
Arnold von Winkelried is a legendary Swiss hero who is supposed to have helped his country to victory over Austria. By seizing as many enemy spears as he could reach and creating a gap in the Austrian lines, he was able to give the Swiss the advantage in the battle of Sempach (1386).

HERALDIC BEASTS
Many Swiss coats of arms are based on animals, like this goat in a stained-glass window at the castle of Chillon.

ON GUARD
The Swiss Guard at the Vatican in Rome have a distinctive coloured uniform.

Flag of Austria

The flag of Austria is in proportions of 2:3. The form used by private citizens is shown here - for official purposes the coat of arms is placed in the centre. The Swiss flag is square, but a civil ensign in proportions of 2:3 was introduced in 1941.

Flag of Switzerland

FOLLOW THE BEAR
This large statue of a bear in the city of Bern is one example of the local emblem.

NATIONAL FLAGS
The flag of Austria is, after that of Denmark, the oldest national flag in the world. One legend says that the design was based on the bloodstained tunic of Duke Leopold V - the only part of the tunic that remained white was the area under his broad belt. The flag of Switzerland, on the other hand, was only adopted officially in 1848.

Italy

HERO OF THE RISORGIMENTO
Garibaldi and his Redshirts started the movement to unite Italy in 1860.

BEFORE 1861, Italy was a collection of many separate states, some ruled by foreign dynasties, others under the control of the Church These all had their own flags and heraldry, and there was no attempt at unity until the end of the eighteenth century. The colours of Italy were established during the great wave of activity when Napoleon invaded Italy in 1796. They were influenced by the French *Tricolore* (pp. 26-27) and were at first used in a horizontal form. The vertical tricolour was introduced in 1798, but was only used until the fall of Napoleon, with whom the flag was so closely associated, in 1802. In 1848, "The Year of Revolutions", they appeared again in the various Italian states. The form adopted by Sardinia eventually became the flag of the new Kingdom of Italy, which was formed in 1861 after Garibaldi united Italy in the movement known as the *Risorgimento* (resurgence). The Kingdom lasted until 1946, when the arms were removed from the flag, which is now a plain tricolour of green, white, and red.

Rome   Papal States

Naples

KEYS OF PETER
These flags were flown by some of the Italian states before 1870. The crossed keys (symbol of St Peter) and the tiara appear on the modern Vatican flag.

GLORY IN BATTLE
Italian soldiers carried the Sardinian version of the tricolour at the battle of Ain-Zara in 1911.

Blue-bordered arms of Savoy

SYMBOLS OF UNITY
The shield and crown of Savoy, combined with Italian flags, formed a popular patriotic symbol.

CAPTURED IN AFRICA
This Italian national flag flew over the citadel of Gondar, Ethiopia, after Italy took over in 1936. It was captured when the emperor reconquered his country, with the help of the British, in 1941.

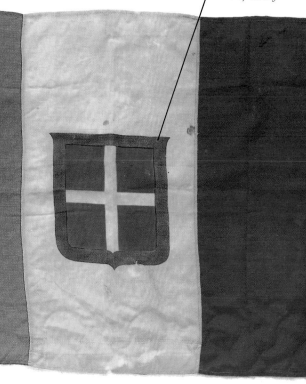

THE LION OF ST MARK
The ancient flag of Venice bore the lion, and a lion flag still flies in St Mark's Square today.

THE ITALIAN TRICOLOUR
The colours of the Italian flag have been interpreted as representing the virutes of Faith, Hope, and Charity, but they are in fact inspired by the French *Tricolore*. They also incorporate the green and white colours of the Milanese militia. There are several variations: the flags used at sea have shields in the centre to distinguish them from the flag of Mexico (p. 60); the naval ensign also has a naval crown above the central shield.

SYMBOL OF THE LEFT
The Italian colours are combined with the hammer and sickle to form the symbol of the Communist Party of Italy.

GROUP OF ALLIES
The British, French, and Italians were allies during World War I. This propaganda picture shows their soldiers and their flags, with the caption "All against the Germans". The Red Ensign (p. 16) has been used to represent Britain, a common mistake at this time.

RACE FOR THE FLAG
Twice a year in Sienna the colourful spectacle of the *Palio* race can be seen. The participants represent the seventeen districts of the city, who compete for the honour of displaying the *Palio* (an ancient flag bearing an image of the Virgin Mary) in their local church. They carry brightly coloured square flags like this.

This lapel badge shows the modern Spanish flag.

Spain and Portugal

ALTHOUGH THEY LOOK VERY DIFFERENT, the flags of Spain and Portugal share a simple two-colour design to which different coats of arms have been added. The colours of Spain, yellow and red, were adopted as recently as 1785, but they have a longer history as the traditional colours of the regions of Castile and Aragon. The yellow-and-red flag was first created during the French Revolutionary Wars (p. 26). Since then, a coat of arms has always appeared on the state flag and ensign. At first the arms of Castile and Leon were used, but in Franco's time (1936-75) they were replaced by the national arms. When the monarchy was restored, the present arms were added, but no arms appear on flags intended for civil use. Portugal adopted a distinctive blue and white flag in 1830. These colours were also traditional, but in 1910 Portugal became a republic, and the colours were changed to red and green.

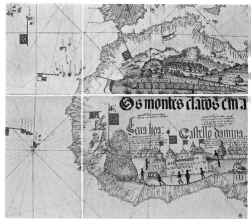

EARLY COLONY
On this map of the Guinea coast (*c.* 1502), an old form of the Portuguese flag is illustrated.

AT SEA
The Spanish colours can be seen in this painting of the Armada (1588).

IN ACTIVE SERVICE
The 1785 version of the Spanish naval ensign is red and yellow with the crowned arms of Castile and Leon. The arms are usually set towards the hoist, so this example has probably lost some material at the fly end while being used.

OLD AND NEW
The 1830 flag of Portugal (left) is strikingly different from the modern flag, although the blue shields are still used. The modern flag of the Azores (right) is derived from the 1830 flag of Portugal. The Azores flag bears a hawk (*açor* in Portuguese).

SPANISH FLAG?
The red-and-yellow flag in this picture is not a Spanish Flag - simply the international signal flag for the letter Y.

Both flags are 2:3 in proportion. The green section of the Portuguese flag accounts for three eighths of the field. In the Spanish flag the yellow stripe is twice the width of the red ones.

Red represents revolution

Green represents Prince Henry the Navigator

Armillary sphere (showing the orbits of the planets), emblem of Henry the Navigator

Flag of Portugal

FLAGS OF TODAY

Although the Spanish national flag is a plain red-and-yellow design, the state and naval flags still include the state arms. The Portuguese, however, use the same flag, complete with coat of arms, for all purposes. In both cases the arms are set nearer the hoist of the flag than the centre. The heraldry of both countries uses the gold castle of Castile; it appears as a border on the Portuguese arms. The blue shields and white discs were known as the *quinas*, and the yellow castles on red were called the "Bordure of Castile".

Five blue shields commemorate Alphonso Henriques, who established Portugal as an independent kingdom

SEPARATISTS' FLAG

The Basque flag, known as the *Ikurrina*, is a frequent sight in the Basque country of northern Spain, especially now that the region has been granted home rule and the flag made official. Its design, with red and green crosses, was inspired by the British Union Flag.

Greece and Balkan

In the 19th century, these two Christian countries struggled to free themselves from the rule of Moslem Turks. Their flags reflect this struggle in different ways. Greece based its symbolism on the cross and Christian banners. The blue and white in the Greek flag derive from an early flag, and from the colours of Bavaria – a prince of that country became the first king of Greece. The nine stripes are thought to derive from the nine syllables of the Greek motto (translated as "Liberty or death"). Whether or not this is true, it shows how closely the flag is linked to the movement for freedom. When Serbia fought for independence in 1912, they used the red, white and blue of Russia, the country which helped them in their victory. These colours became known as the "Pan-Slav" colours. When the Federal Socialist Republic of Yugoslavia was formed, the red star of Communism was added to the flag. Four of the former Yugoslav republics became independent states in 1992.

This figure represents the 19th-century idea of Greek elegance and beauty

FLAGS FOR FREEDOM
In 1992, the Yugoslav republics regained their independence. In Croatia, the ancient arms of red and white were revived.

STAMPS OF CHANGE
On the day Slovenia became independent, stamps with the new arms were issued. They show Mount Triglav, and a wavy line representing rivers and coasts.

SYMBOL OF DIVISION
The Croatian flag is hoisted to indicate the new state's frontier. The disputes over the division of Yugoslavia led to the bloodiest war in Europe since World War II.

Greek colours at the Royal Palace, Athens

HERO OF THE GREEKS
The poet Lord Byron was a passionate supporter of Greek independence, and took part in the struggles of the 1820s. He died in Greece, at Missolonghi, in April 1824 and became a Greek national hero.

EARLY GREEK FLAG
This Greek postage stamp shows an early Greek national flag. The traditional Greek colours have a long history of use.

Cross recalls
religious origins
of the freedom
movement

The Greek flag is in proportions of 7:12.
The blue of the flag has varied over
the years. It is now a bright
intermediate shade.
The porportions of the Yugoslav
flag are 1:2, but the merchant flag is 2:3.

Flag of Greece

Flag of Yugoslavia (Serbia
and Montenegro)

Flag no longer has a red
star emblem in the centre

NATIONAL FLAGS

The design of the Greek flag is inspired by the
American Stars and Stripes, but incorporates the
Christian symbol of the cross. The layout of the
stripes in the Yugoslav flag dates from 1918,
when Serbia and the other Yugoslav states
formed a united kingdom. Until the time of the
German occupation, the national flag consisted
of a plain tricolour. Tito placed the red star in
the centre at the start of Communist rule, and the
flags of the constituent republics also acquired
red stars. Following the breakup of the federation
in 1992, two states, Serbia and Montenegro, kept
the name Yugoslavia and kept the flag, but
removed the Communist red star.

MEETING OF ALLIES

This picture of a pro-allied
demonstration in Salonika
during 1916 shows the Greek
flag, together with those of
Italy, France, the
Netherlands, and the
British Red Ensign.

Denmark

THE DANES HAVE one of the oldest flags still in use, and there are two different stories of its origin. According to legend, the red flag with a white cross fell from heaven in 1219 during a battle at which the Christian Danes were victorious over the pagan Estonians. But according to historical records, the flag first appeared in the arms of King Valdemar Atterdag in the fourteenth century. At that time the cross had arms of equal length, like the cross of St George (p. 47), but over the years the outer arm lengthened to produce the characteristic "Scandinavian" cross. As with the English flag of St George, the colours of the cross are not those of the royal arms. This may be because the red and white flag was in general use in Christian Europe, since it can also be found in several other countries. The Danish cross and flag form spread to other Scandinavian countries and to Finland and Germany; it can also be found in Normandy, a memento of the days when Norsemen colonized Europe. The Danes themselves are great flag-flyers, and the Danish flag can be seen in a variety of settings in Denmark - from government buildings and town halls to back gardens and Christmas trees.

The Danish flag on a 19th-century Christmas card.

EARLY ORIGINS
The Danish flag first appeared on the arms of King Valdemar IV Atterdag (1340-75). The royal shield is the same today.

SPLITFLAG
This early 15th-century seal shows the swallowtail version of the Danish flag, called the Splitflag. It is used for naval and official purposes.

Dragoon standard from the reign of Christian IV (1588-1648).

Musketeer company flag from the reign of Christian VII (1766-1808) used in the Napoleonic War.

Infantry flag from the reign of Christian IV(1588-1648).

ARMY FLAGS
Denmark has a strong tradition of military flags. Many include the Danish cross. The infantry flag has the national flag in the canton, and the device of a mailed fist emerging from a cloud, dealing out thunderbolts. The motto is "Terror to the Enemy". The Musketeer flag also uses the Danish cross, while the Dragoon flag has a classical image of victory.

FLAG OF THE FAROES
The Faroe Islands have had their own flag since 1931, with a design based on the flags of Denmark and Iceland. The flag became official, for use on land only, in 1948.

MODERN COLOURS
Flags of the military units of today are generally based on the Danish national flag.

Inner cantons are
three-sevenths of
width

The flag is in proportions of 28:37, which
were laid down in 1848. The naval flag is
somewhat longer (56:107). The width of the
cross is one-seventh of the width of the flag.
For official purposes badges are often placed
in the canton, or in the centre of the cross.

THE DANNEBROG

The Danish flag is known as the
Dannebrog, or "Danish cloth".
Although it is a very old design, its
precise proportions were only laid
down in 1848. Its design has given rise
to the flags of Norway, Iceland, the
Faroe Islands, and probably also to
those of Sweden and Finland. But the
exact proportions of the flag and the
cross are unlike those of any other
country.

Beer-can illustration showing Danish
flags flying on allotments

FLYING THE FLAG

The Danes are proud of the
Dannebrog and display it
everywhere. It even appears
in peoples' private gardens
and allotments (left) and is
sometimes used by the young
as a pattern for make-up
(above).

IN THE POLAR WASTES

Greenland, a part of Denmark that has home
rule, acquired its own flag for use on land and at
sea in 1985. The design was the winning entry in
a competition. In the Danish colours, it
represents the sun rising over the polar ice.

Norway and Iceland

THE FLAGS of Norway and Iceland are very similar. They have a common origin because both designs are based on that of the flag of Denmark, the country to which both nations belonged. The flag of Norway was designed in 1821 after control of the country had passed to Sweden. The blue cross was added so that the colours were the same as those of the French tricolour. In the nineteenth century there was a struggle to get this flag accepted for use at sea and on land without any "union" markings symbolizing Norway's link with Sweden. This was only achieved in 1899 and led to the dissolution of the union with Sweden in 1905. In the Icelandic flag the blue and white are said to come from the colours of the Order of the Silver Falcon. The flag was created in 1913, and was allowed to be used at sea after 1918, when Iceland became a separate realm of the Danish crown. When the island became an independent republic in 1944, the flag became the national flag.

SUPERB STANDARD
This ornate flag is a cavalry standard made in the city of Trondheim in the late 17th century. It is richly embroidered on a red damask fabric. Its shape recalls some of the European military guidons (pp. 12–13), which are also elaborately decorated.

Cavalry standard

ENEMY AT THE GATES
Both these Norwegian flags - a cavalry standard and a regimental colour - date from the 17th century. They both bear the arms of Norway, a lion holding a long-handled axe. In the corner of the cavalry standard is the cross of Denmark, to which Norway belonged until 1814. The regimental colour is that of Hannibal Sehested's regiment and bears his motto "Hannibal is at the gates".

Cavalry standard

Regimental colour

CONQUERING THE POLE
The Norwegian flag has the distinction of being the first at the South Pole, which was reached by Captain Roald Amundsen on 14 December 1911. It took Amundsen and his four companions 55 days to reach the Pole, using skis and sleds pulled by dogs to transport their supplies. They left the Norwegian flag in the ice and it was still there when Captain Scott, Amundsen's British rival, reached the South Pole a month later.

SWALLOW-TAIL
The naval ensign of Iceland takes a distinctive swallow-tailed form. The custom of using this shape for naval and official purposes is common in Scandinavia.

ÍSLAND 50 KR

The flag of Norway is made in proportions of 8:11. The proportions of the Icelandic flag are 18:25. The inner cantons of the Norwegian flag are half the length of the outer ones.

Narrow inner canton

Fimbriation

Flag of Norway

Fimbriation

Flag of Iceland

NATIONAL FLAGS
In the flag of Norway the cross and its surrounding fimbriation are one quarter the width of the flag, whereas in the Icelandic flag they are wider. Both countries use swallow-tailed versions of their flags, but those of Norway have an extension of the cross as well, forming a tongue, as used in Sweden and Finland. Badges can be placed in the canton or in the centre of the cross.

Sweden and Finland

SWEDISH ARMS
Flags and heraldry have a long history in Sweden. The three crowns of the medieval state arms are shown here. This Swedish soldier also carries a very long lance-pennon (p. 6).

A Swedish knight of the 14th century covered with heraldic emblems

FINLAND WAS PART OF SWEDEN from the twelfth century until 1809, but never lost its individual character. In 1809 it became part of the Russian Empire and in 1917 it finally achieved independence, joining the Scandinavian group of nations. Both Sweden and Finland have national flags based on the Scandinavian cross. In the case of Sweden the colours are derived from the traditional arms, and in Finland they are based on the blue and white used in the nineteenth century to represent the blue lakes and white snows of the country. The Swedish cross dates back to at least 1533, although the arms with their gold crowns on a blue background date back to 1364. As in Denmark, flags form an important part of Swedish life, and a national flag day is celebrated on 6 June each year. Finland's arms were granted by King John of Sweden in 1581. They include a lion treading on a scimitar (a common Moslem symbol), representing victory over enemies from the east, and nine roses, which stand for the country's nine provinces.

GUSTAVUS VASA
King Gustav I of Sweden reigned from 1496 to 1560 and was a member of the House of Vasa. He fought for Sweden against the Danes, whom he eventually defeated in 1523. He is remembered as a just and pious king.

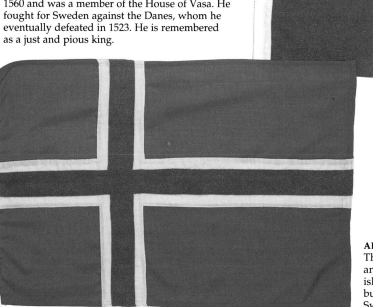

SCANIA
This region in southern Sweden has tried to secure home rule and has a flag that is well known in Sweden. Scania was ruled by Denmark until 1658, and the colours of the flag are derived from those of Denmark and Sweden.

ALAND ISLANDS
This flag dates from the 1920s and represents a group of islands that belong to Finland but are inhabited mainly by Swedes. The colours combine the blue and yellow of Sweden with the red and yellow of the islands' arms.

The traditional arms of Sweden on a military standard

Flag of Sweden

Flag of Finland

NATIONAL FLAGS

During the union with Norway (1814-1905), the flag of Sweden had a "union mark" in the canton. Modern flags date from the Flag Law of 1906. The flag of Finland evolved in the nineteenth century, but was only chosen officially in 1918. The blue and white colours first appeared in 1860 and various designs were suggested before the Scandinavian cross proved triumphant.

NAVAL VERSION

The Swedes use this shape of flag for ships. The Swedish royal flag has a similar shape with the royal arms in the centre.

SUOMI FINLAND 10,00

FINNISH ARMS

This postage stamp shows the coat of arms of Finland, with the lion treading on a scimitar and nine roses.

The United Kingdom

SINCE THE THIRTEENTH CENTURY, the English have flown a flag bearing the red cross of St George, the country's patron saint. This was the flag behind which they rode into battle on the seventh crusade, although they also carried flags bearing the English royal arms, with their heraldic lions and gold *fleur de lys* (p. 26). At about the same time the Scottish adopted the saltire cross of St Andrew, a white cross on a blue background, as their flag. When the two kingdoms were united in 1606, these two crosses were combined to produce one of the most striking flag designs - the Union Flag. When Ireland was united with Great Britain in 1801 the red cross of St Patrick was incorporated into the design, to produce the flag we know today. The fourth country of the United Kingdom, Wales, is not represented in the Union Flag, although the Welsh have their own flag, bearing a red dragon on a white and green field.

ROYAL FUNERAL
The banners of England, Ireland, Wales, Chester, and Cornwall decorated the funeral train of Queen Elizabeth I.

DEATH IN BATTLE
This painting of the death of Major Pierson at the battle of St Helier, Jersey shows the pre-1801 version of the Union Flag.

Plain white diagonals show that this flag was made before 1801. Badly aligned diagonals are a common mistake in flag-making; this flag was probably made aboard ship

SAVING THE COLOURS
These British Guards are saving their colours at the Battle of Inkerman in the Crimean War. Troops made every effort to prevent colours being captured.

EARLY VERSION
Lord Howe's command flag was flown on his ship HMS Queen Charlotte at the Battle of the First of June, 1794.

Red hand is the traditional emblem of Ulster

CARRYING THE COLOURS
The "ensign" was the most junior officer of a regiment. He carried the colours, and took his title from them. This 19th-century painting shows an ensign of the 75th Highlanders Regiment.

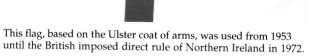

This flag, based on the Ulster coat of arms, was used from 1953 until the British imposed direct rule of Northern Ireland in 1972.

Although the union with Ireland was dissolved in 1921 St Patrick's cross still remains in the flag

White diagonals for Scotland

Blue background for Scotland

White background for England

There are no official specifications for the construction of the flag. It is usually made in proportions of 1:2, but the colours can be any shades of red and blue.

England

Scotland

Ireland

THREE FLAGS IN ONE
The English cross of St George and the Scottish Saltire are still very widely used, although the cross of St Patrick is now largely super-seded by the flags of Ulster (see opposite) and Eire (p. 61).

THE "UNION JACK"
Although its correct name is the Union Flag, the British national flag is usually known as the Union Jack. A jack is a small flag flown from the jackstaff at the bow of a ship, but the Union Jack is only used in this way by the Queen. It is flown on the mainmast by the Admiral of the Fleet. The Union Jack is the national flag for use on land. It is also used by the Commander in Chief of the British army.

FLAG AS FASHION
In the 1960s the Union Jack was used on clothes and other items.

FLAG FOR HIGH FLIERS
This special ensign was produced for the Royal Air Force at the time of the Armistice celebrations in 1918. The modern RAF ensign was introduced some two years later.

BRITISH BULLDOG
During the Boer War and World War I the Union Jack was used widely as a patriotic symbol.

Canada and New Zealand

ARMS OF NEW ZEALAND
The arms have the Southern Cross in the main quarter. The royal crown replaced the previous crest in 1953. The supporters carry a New Zealand flag and a Maori spear. Around the scroll are leaves of fern, the national badge.

CANADA WAS THE FIRST DOMINION to be set up within the British Empire, but the last to adopt a distinctive flag. New Zealand, on the other hand, had its own local ensign even before it became part of the Empire. Under British influence, Maori chiefs chose the "Waitangi" flag in 1834, and used it until 1840, when they handed over control of New Zealand to Queen Victoria. After this, New Zealand used British ensigns with various badges, until the four stars of the Southern Cross (pp. 50-1) were adopted in 1896. The form of the Southern Cross used in New Zealand is similar to that on the Australian flag, but has only four stars. They were originally red on a white disc and when the red stars were placed on the fly of the Blue Ensign, they were outlined in white, so that they could be seen more clearly. Canada also used British ensigns after it became a Federal Dominion in 1867. In 1892 the use of a shield of arms on the Red Ensign was authorized for use at sea, and after 1945 this became the form used on land as well. In 1965 the present design was introduced, using the maple leaf, which had been an emblem of Canada since the nineteenth century. It was only adopted after the longest parliamentary debate in Canadian history. The provinces of Canada also developed ensign badges. Newfoundland did the same, and had its own set of ensigns before 1949, when it became part of Canada.

Bicentennial badge from the province of Ontario, Canada (1784-1984)

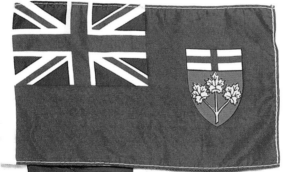

BRITISH BANNER
A British Red Ensign with the provincial shield in the fly makes up the flag of Ontario. The shield, with its yellow maple leaves, dates from 1868, and the flag was made official in 1965. It emphasizes the British link with Canada.

BRITISH LINKS
The Red Ensign with the Canadian shield was used by Canada in both World Wars. The Canadian State Arms still include the Union Jack.

FOR THE FRENCH
Known as the *fleurdelysé* flag, the banner of Québec derives from an earlier 19th-century version, and represents French-speakers throughout Canada. The *fleur de lys* and the white cross on blue recall the flags of pre-revolutionary France (p. 26).

SUN IN SPLENDOUR
The device of the setting sun on the British Columbian banner refers to the province's geographical position as the westernmost state, and also to the motto on its arms: *Splendor sine Occasu* ("A splendour that never sets").

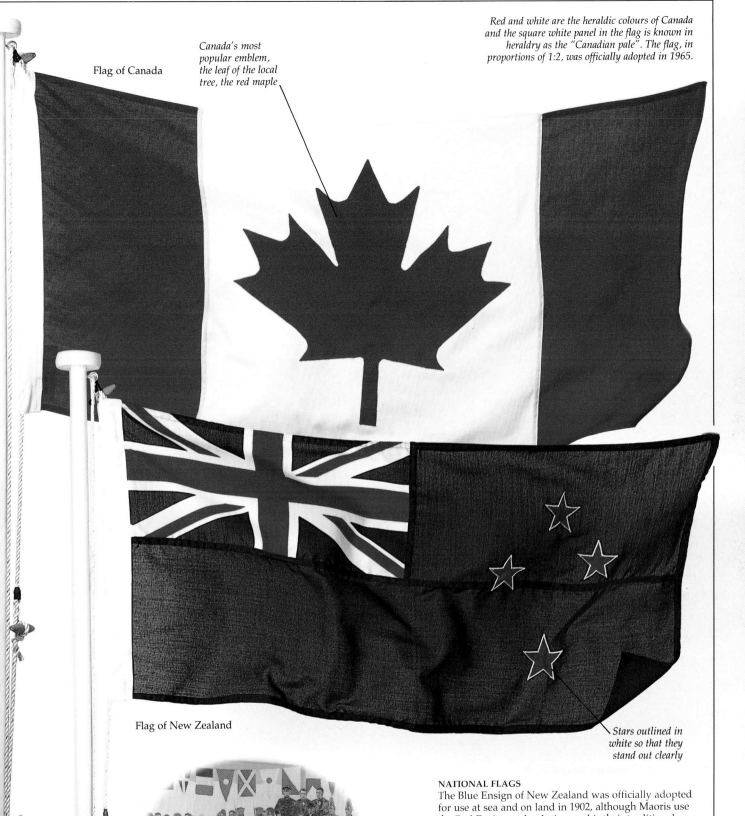

Flag of Canada

Canada's most
popular emblem,
the leaf of the local
tree, the red maple

Red and white are the heraldic colours of Canada
and the square white panel in the flag is known in
heraldry as the "Canadian pale". The flag, in
proportions of 1:2, was officially adopted in 1965.

Flag of New Zealand

Stars outlined in
white so that they
stand out clearly

HANDING OVER
The Treaty of Waitangi (1840) turned the
Maoris into British subjects.

NATIONAL FLAGS
The Blue Ensign of New Zealand was officially adopted
for use at sea and on land in 1902, although Maoris use
the Red Ensign on land, since red is their traditional
colour. With the adoption of the distinctive Canadian
flag in 1965, Australia, New Zealand, Fiji, and Tuvalu
are the only countries of the British Commonwealth
whose flags still include the Union Jack. The flag of
Canada includes the leaf of the maple, a familiar tree
in Canada and a Canadian symbol with a long history.
The flag may be used both at sea and on land.

Australia

THE SOUTHERN CROSS, the bright constellation visible from the southern hemisphere that has been used for centuries by sailors as a navigational aid, has been a major theme in Australian symbolism since the early nineteenth century. The first flag to carry the four stars of the Southern Cross was the National Colonial Flag of 1823-4, which placed them on the red cross of the British White Ensign. In 1831 the New South Wales ensign appeared, very similar to the Commonwealth Flag (see below), but with stars of eight points. In due course this became the "Federation" flag. In 1854 the Eureka Stockade flag appeared, and there were several other adaptations of the emblem, including the ensign badge of Victoria (1870). So it is not surprising that the Southern Cross figured in the design which won the competition for a flag after Australia became a federal dominion in 1901. The resulting flag consisted of the Southern Cross on a blue field, with the Union Jack in the canton. The stars are not quite the same as those in the flag of Victoria, and their varying numbers of points indicate the brilliance of the actual stars. The flag also had a large star of six points, standing for the six states. This was altered to a seven-pointed star in 1908, so that the Northern Territory of Australia was also represented.

DISCOVERER OF TASMANIA
In 1642 Abel Tasman discovered the island that now bears his name (it was formerly "Van Diemen's Land"). He was exploring on behalf of the Dutch East India Company and his ship carried their tricolour flag.

THE EUREKA FLAG
This flag originally represented the Ballarat Reform League of 1854, which tried to redress the grievances of the gold miners, who were fighting for a fairer licensing system for mining and for electoral reforms. It was hoisted over the stockade where the miners resisted the state troopers. Although the protest was quickly overwhelmed by the soldiers, a Reform League was established to examine disputes between the miners and the government. The reputation of the Eureka Stockade as a focus for radical ideas has lived on, and the flag is still popular in Australia, particularly as a republican symbol.

Stars could have five or eight points

Design derives from flag of New South Wales (1831)

FLAG FOR UNITY
The "Federation" flag stood for the idea of uniting the six Australian states as an independent nation, which was not achieved until 1 January 1901. During the last two decades of the 19th century the Australian Natives Association and the Australian Federation League popularized the idea by displaying this flag.

BOUNCING BACK
One of these boomerangs is decorated with motifs from the Australian flag.

Union Jack signifies the link with Britain and the Commonwealth

"Crux Australis" (the Southern Cross)

Commonwealth Star

WINNING DESIGN

A total of 32,823 designs were entered for the competition to find a flag for Australia in 1900. Five separate entrants submitted the winning design, which was officially adopted in February 1903 for use on Australian vessels, and became the legal national flag in April 1954. The flag design consists of three parts: the Union Jack (showing the link with Britain), the Southern Cross (for Australia) and the Commonwealth Star (for the federal system). The official national colours of Australia, however, are green and yellow, and many of the new proposals for Australian flags use these colours.

New South Wales

Queensland

Western Australia

South Australia

Tasmania

Victoria

ABORIGINAL LAND RIGHTS FLAG

This flag has become a powerful symbol for the native people of Australia. Black represents the people, the yellow circle stands for the sun, and the red is for the land of Australia.

STATE FLAGS

Each of Australia's six states has a flag, based on the British Blue Ensign, with the relevant flag-badge in the fly. The badges are derived from the states' coats of arms. Recently South Australia changed its arms to the same design as the flag-badge. Each

state governor also has a flag. The flags date from the following years: 1875 (Tasmania, Western Australia), 1876 (New South Wales, Queensland), 1877 (Victoria) and 1904 (South Australia). The Northern Territory also has its own flag.

Japan

A 19th-century western view of a Japanese woman.

THE NAME JAPAN means "source of the sun". This fact is clearly reflected in Japanese flag design, for the two best known forms of the Japanese flag are the red sun-disc on a white field (the national flag of today), and the "Rising Sun", which has red rays extending from the sun to the edge of the flag. For centuries, Japan was virtually a "closed" country, shunning all foreign influence and doing without a national flag. However, the sun-disc design is an old one, and was revived after the visit of the American Commodore Perry in 1853, when Japan finally opened its doors to the influence of the West. First it was used as a national ensign, and it was legalized on 27 February 1870, following the Meiji Restoration of 1868, when the powerful Shogun was overthrown and the Emperor reclaimed his political power. The flag's name in Japanese is *Hinomaru*, the sun-disc flag.

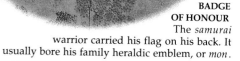

BADGE OF HONOUR
The *samurai* warrior carried his flag on his back. It usually bore his family heraldic emblem, or *mon*.

FLAG WITH PHOENIXES
Captured from the Japanese by the British in 1945, this flag includes two phoenixes surrounding a heraldic emblem or *mon*. In eastern thought the phoenix symbolizes the sun. This device can be seen today on the flag of the President of South Korea.

THE RISING SUN
This flag was adopted as the naval and military ensign on 3 November 1889, but was outlawed at the end of the World War II. However, it was revived for the Maritime Defence Force in June 1954 and forms the basis for the rank flags of Admirals. A flag with the same basic design is used today for the "Ground Self-Defence Force". This example is from the World War II.

*Proportions 1:2
(modern version is 2:3)*

Phoenix represents the sun

VICTORY!
The Rising Sun ensign flew on the Japanese ships at the battle of Tsushima, 1905, when the Japanese defeated a Russian fleet.

52

THE SUN-DISC FLAG

One of the simplest national flags, the sun-disc was first hoisted at sea in 1855, carried to America in 1860, and made the basis of regimental colours in 1870. It was approved for private use in 1872. The white ground is said to stand for purity and integrity and the red disc for sincerity, brightness, and warmth, and so the flag symbolizes the Japanese ideal of *Akaki kiyoki tadashiki naoki makoto no kokoro* ("Bright, pure, just and of gentle heart").

Inscription radiates from centre of flag

SOLDIER'S PRAYERS

During World War II soldiers carried flags inscribed with prayers, often made for them by their families. The prayers were never written on the sun-disc itself. Many such flags ended up as souvenirs in enemy hands.

IN HONOUR OF THE EMPEROR

Flags are often used on feast days and holidays. In fact the Japanese sign for a holiday is two crossed flags. Here the flag is used to greet the Emperor, who has his own personal flag bearing the chrysanthemum *mon* in gold on red.

Africa and South America

THE FLAGS OF THESE CONTINENTS have emerged from periods of revolution and emancipation. The peoples of Spanish America began to throw off the rule of Spain in the early years of the nineteenth century, with the help of soldiers such as Miranda of Venezuela , Bolivar of Bolivia, and San Martin of Argentina. Not surprisingly, many of their flags were tricolours, inspired by the French revolutionary flag and using colours associated with these national heroes. Many of these tricolours still form the basis of the national flags of Latin America. In Africa the process of gaining independence was the work of lawyers and politicians such as Nkrumah of Ghana and Kenyatta of Kenya. In designing their flags, the people of the new African nations looked to the example of Ethiopia, a country that had avoided foreign rule for many years. The Ethiopian flag of green, yellow, and red had been adopted by the West Indians and combined with the colours of Marcus Garvey (p.25) to make the well-known Rastafarian combination. Ghana became the first African state to adopt these colours, in 1957, since when they have become widespread.

BIRDS OF A FEATHER
Mexico makes use of Aztec traditions in its arms, which depict the legend of the foundation of Mexico city. These arms appear on the tricolour flag of Mexico.

ALL CHANGE
A new country, a new stamp, a new flag. Gambia's flag was adopted in 1965.

IN THE VANGUARD
The Ethiopian flag flew at the Battle of Lasta during the Ethiopian civil war.

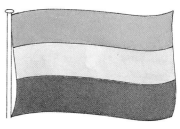

RASTAFARIAN COLOURS
The flag of Ethiopia emerged in the 1890s. It was the inspiration of the Rastafarians, the members of the West Indian cult who, rejecting western culture and ideas, regard Haile Selassie, the former Ethiopian emperor, as divine. Ethiopia remained free of colonization until 1936 and won admiration for its resistance.

FLAG OF CONFLICT
This marker flag was used by the King's African Rifles during the campaign against the Mau Mau movement in Kenya. This movement aimed to gain better conditions for Africans under British rule, and the struggles between the two sides led eventually to the demand for independence from Britain. The figure 3 in the flag stands for the 3rd platoon. The flag's crude manufacture suggests that it was locally made.

PRIDE OF KENYA
Peter Rono, Olympic gold medal winner at Seoul, carries the flag of Kenya. It is based on the Garvey colours admired by Jomo Kenyatta, the "father" of modern Kenya.

Map of Brazil

Thirteen stripes, like flag of United States

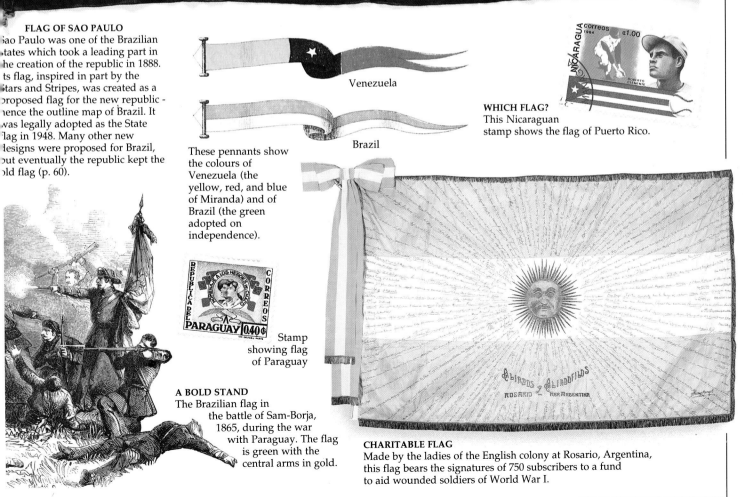

FLAG OF SAO PAULO
Sao Paulo was one of the Brazilian states which took a leading part in the creation of the republic in 1888. Its flag, inspired in part by the Stars and Stripes, was created as a proposed flag for the new republic - hence the outline map of Brazil. It was legally adopted as the State flag in 1948. Many other new designs were proposed for Brazil, but eventually the republic kept the old flag (p. 60).

Venezuela

Brazil

These pennants show the colours of Venezuela (the yellow, red, and blue of Miranda) and of Brazil (the green adopted on independence).

WHICH FLAG?
This Nicaraguan stamp shows the flag of Puerto Rico.

Stamp showing flag of Paraguay

A BOLD STAND
The Brazilian flag in the battle of Sam-Borja, 1865, during the war with Paraguay. The flag is green with the central arms in gold.

CHARITABLE FLAG
Made by the ladies of the English colony at Rosario, Argentina, this flag bears the signatures of 750 subscribers to a fund to aid wounded soldiers of World War I.

Russia

MEETING OF ALLIES
This painting commem-
orating the alliance
between France and
Russia in 1893 shows
several pre-
revolutionary flags.

BEFORE THE RUSSIAN REVOLUTION in 1917, the person who had the greatest influ-ence over the flags of Russia was the emperor, Peter the Great. Among his other innovations, Peter founded a navy and endowed it with flags and ensigns. These were based on Dutch models and used the colours red, white, and blue. These colours had been used on flags before his reign, but he was the first to establish and arrange a complete set of naval flags using these colours. Several other eastern European countries followed suit and adopted red, white and blue flags. Many other flags were used in Russia before the revolution. During World War I, for example, the civil flag had a yellow canton with the Imperial arms, but this was dropped before the revolution, when the red flag of the Bolsheviks took over. During the revolution red flags with inscriptions were widely used; more orthodox ones were intro-duced once the new regime was established.

PETER THE GREAT
The emperor reigned from 1682 to 1725. He founded a navy and created the flags of Imperial Russia.

TO EACH HIS OWN
Before and after the revolution Russia had flags for every office and department of government. A selection is shown here. 1 Fleet Auxiliaries. 2 Finnish Customs Posts. 3 Customs Service. 4 Vice-Admiral. 5 Chief of Naval staff. 6 Port Commander. 7 Minister of War. 8 Hydrographic Service. 9 Royal Prince as General-Admiral. 10 Czarevich as General-Admiral. 11 General-Admiral.

1   2   3

4   5   6   7

8   9   10   11

OFF TO THE WAR
General Dragomiroff, who left Russia for the war against Japan in 1904, kissed the Russian flag as a sign of allegiance. Pictures of soldiers kissing the flag were popular patriotic images (p. 28).

RED ON SILVER
Diplomats often attach flags to cars they use abroad, for instant recognition. Here, the red flag of the former Soviet Union flies from the "Silver Lady" of an English Rolls Royce.

THE HAMMER AND SICKLE
Following the Russian Revolution, the Union of Soviet Socialist Republics (USSR) was formed and remained in existence from 1922 until the Union break-up of 1991. The 15 republics in the Union all used red flags based on the national flag, introduced in 1923. The hammer and sickle represented the workers in industry and agriculture, and the red star the guiding light of the Communist Party.

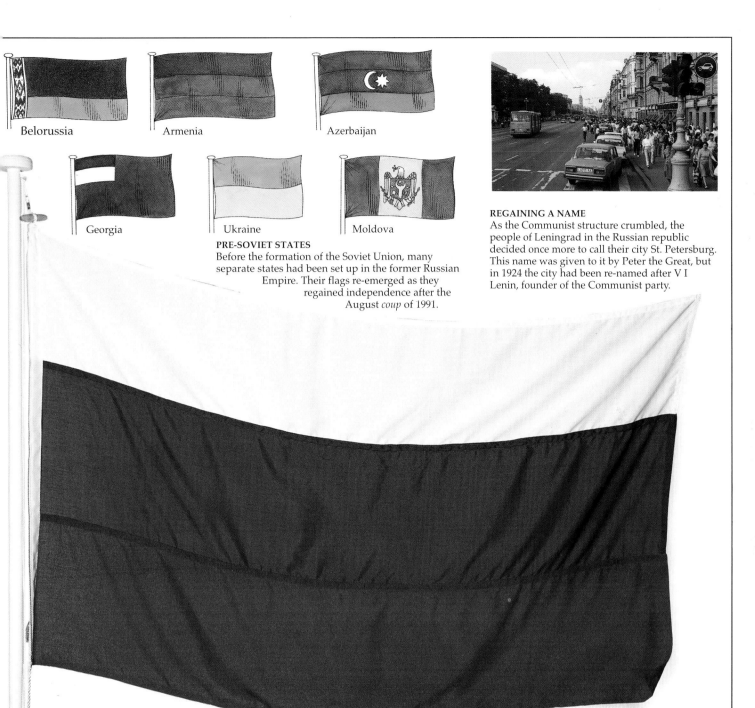

Belorussia

Armenia

Azerbaijan

Georgia

Ukraine

Moldova

PRE-SOVIET STATES
Before the formation of the Soviet Union, many separate states had been set up in the former Russian Empire. Their flags re-emerged as they regained independence after the August *coup* of 1991.

REGAINING A NAME
As the Communist structure crumbled, the people of Leningrad in the Russian republic decided once more to call their city St. Petersburg. This name was given to it by Peter the Great, but in 1924 the city had been re-named after V I Lenin, founder of the Communist party.

Tajikistan

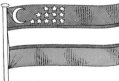

Uzbekistan

Kyrgyzstan

Symbol of the sun and the felt tents of ancient nomads

CENTRAL ASIAN RENAISSANCE
The five states of central Asia are Moslem, but did not exist in their present boundaries until they became part of the Russian empire. Now they are fully independent, all their emblems are new.

RETURN OF THE TRICOLOUR
Following the *coup* and the disintegration of the USSR into independent states, the white, blue and red tricolour was re-adopted by Russia.

Turkmenistan

Kazakhstan

Latvia

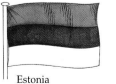

Estonia

Lithuania

BALTIC STATES
The independence of the three Baltic states was recognised immediately after the *coup*. The flags which they had used before being forced into the Soviet Union were displayed once more.

China

ALL ABOARD
This Chinaman carries the flag of the main Chinese shipping line, probably the Chinese flag most often seen by foreigners before 1911.

IN CHINESE THOUGHT the world is divided into five parts, the centre (coloured yellow), the south (red), the north (black), the west (white), and the east (blue). Each part has its own symbol - the dragon, for example, represents the east. So when in 1872 the Chinese at last adopted a national flag, it was natural that it should be yellow, for the "Middle Kingdom", and bear the Blue Dragon of the East. Yellow was also the colour of the Manchu dynasty. In 1911, when revolutionaries within the army took over, the main flag took the form of five simple stripes in the traditional colours. This remained in use until 1928, when the flag of the Kuo Min Tang party was adopted; it represented a white sun in blue sky over red land. This flag is still in use in Taiwan (p. 63), but was replaced on the mainland in 1949 by the red flag of the Peoples' Republic.

EARLY ADVERTISEMENTS
Chinese traders' banners have carried inscriptions for centuries, as these examples show.

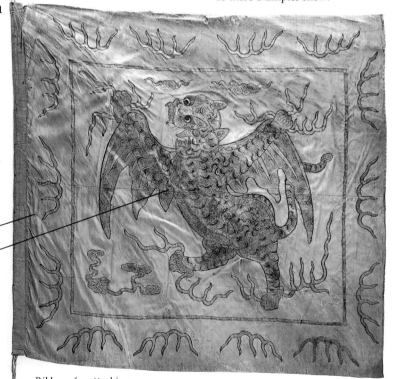

Cream silk

Painted figures

DRAGON OF THE EAST
This beautifully embroidered flag was the first form of the Chinese national flag, used from 1872 to 1890. The device of the blue dragon snapping at the sun was later used on a rectangular flag. The size of the flag varied with the size of the vessel, and could be up to 3 m (10 ft) long at the base.

Hand-embroidered silk

Ribbons for attaching flag to mast

The second form of the Chinese flag is shown in this image dating from 1894.

BURNING BRIGHT
The winged tiger appeared on several military flags captured by the British during their campaign in China in 1857. Its claws hold lightning flashes and the border represents tongues of flame. The divisions of the Chinese army were known as "Banners".

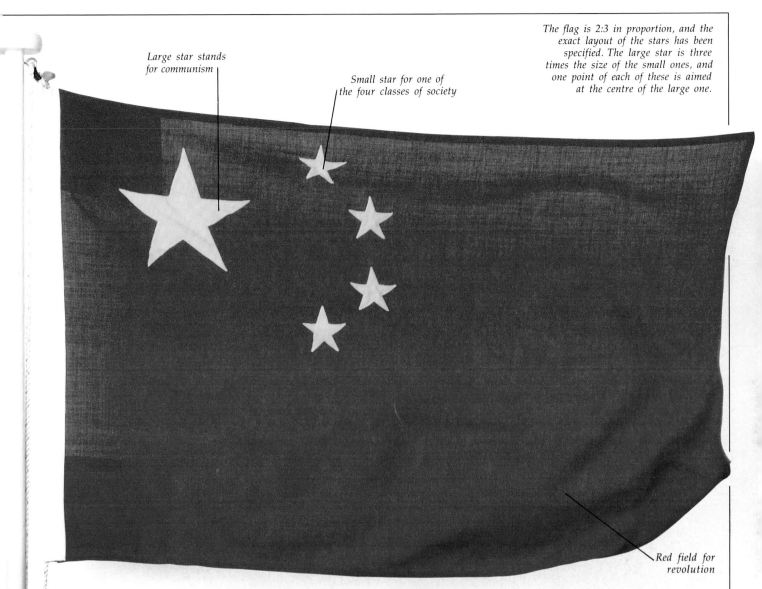

Large star stands for communism

Small star for one of the four classes of society

The flag is 2:3 in proportion, and the exact layout of the stars has been specified. The large star is three times the size of the small ones, and one point of each of these is aimed at the centre of the large one.

Red field for revolution

THE FLAG OF REVOLUTION
The red of the flag adopted in 1949 represents revolution, but also recalls the colour of the Han people. Of the five stars, the large one represents communism, while the four small ones stand for the workers, peasants, bourgeoisie, and "patriotic capitalists".

JUNK FLAG
This early version of the dragon flag was taken from a Chinese junk during the Opium Wars in the 19th century.

Linen hoist with tie-ribbons

FORCES FOR CHANGE *above*
This postage stamp shows the flag of the Chinese Liberation Army. The characters on the flag stand for 1-8, representing 1 August 1928, the date of the army's formation.

ON THE MARCH
Sailors march through Beijing carrying large, plain red flags.

Indented edge typical of Chinese flags

Flags of all nations

FLAGS OF THE WORLD
This illustration shows the variety of flags in use in the 19th century.

TODAY'S NATIONAL FLAGS have a great variety of designs. On the following pages, 160 of the most interesting are shown, arranged by continent. There are many similarities between the different flags. A number of African countries use the colours red, yellow, green, and black, often known as "Pan-African colours". Arab countries often use red, white, black, and green. There are also flags derived from the French *Tricolore*, from the Stars and Stripes, and from the Crescent and Star flag of Turkey. National flags vary in shape, from the square Swiss flag to the long, thin flag of Qatar.

AMERICA

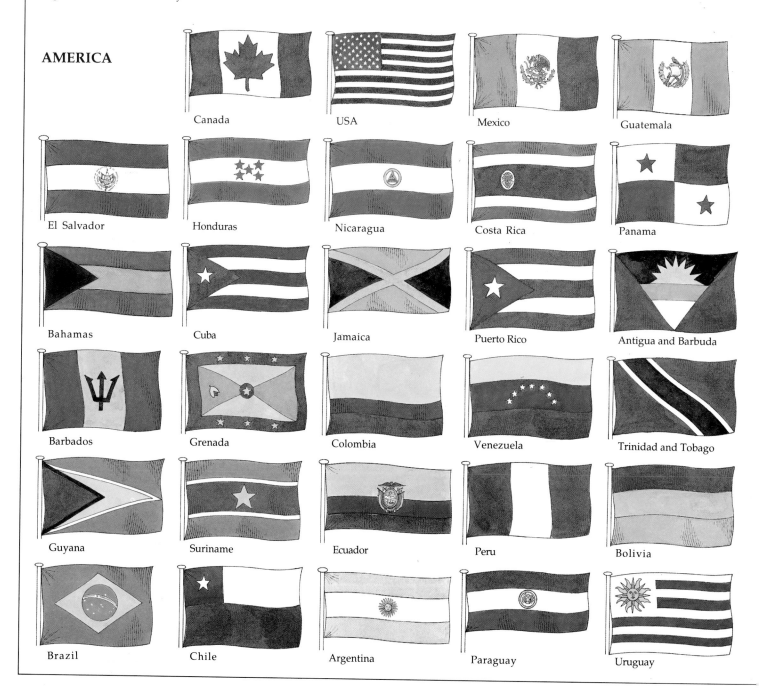

Canada

USA

Mexico

Guatemala

El Salvador

Honduras

Nicaragua

Costa Rica

Panama

Bahamas

Cuba

Jamaica

Puerto Rico

Antigua and Barbuda

Barbados

Grenada

Colombia

Venezuela

Trinidad and Tobago

Guyana

Suriname

Ecuador

Peru

Bolivia

Brazil

Chile

Argentina

Paraguay

Uruguay

EUROPE

Iceland

Ireland

United Kingdom

Denmark

Norway

Sweden

Finland

France

Belgium

Luxembourg

Netherlands

Germany

Malta

Switzerland

Liechtenstein

Austria

Czech Republic

Poland

Russia

Portugal

Spain

Ukraine

Italy

Yugoslavia

Hungary

Albania

Romania

Bulgaria

Greece

AFRICA

Morocco

Algeria

Tunisia

Libya

Egypt

Western Sahara

Mauritania

Mali

Burkina Faso

Niger

Chad

Sudan

Ethiopia

Djibouti

Somalia

Senegal

Gambia

Guinea-Bissau

Guinea

Sierra Leone

Liberia

Ivory Coast

Ghana

Togo

Benin

Nigeria

Cameroon

Central African Rep.

Equatorial Guinea

Gabon

Congo

Democratic Rep.
of Congo (Zaire)

Uganda

Kenya

Namibia

Burundi

Tanzania

Angola

Zambia

Malawi

Mozambique

Comoros

Botswana

Zimbabwe

South Africa

Lesotho

Swaziland

Madagascar

Mauritius

ASIA

Turkey

Israel

Lebanon

Syria

Jordan

Iraq

Saudi Arabia

Kuwait

Bahrain

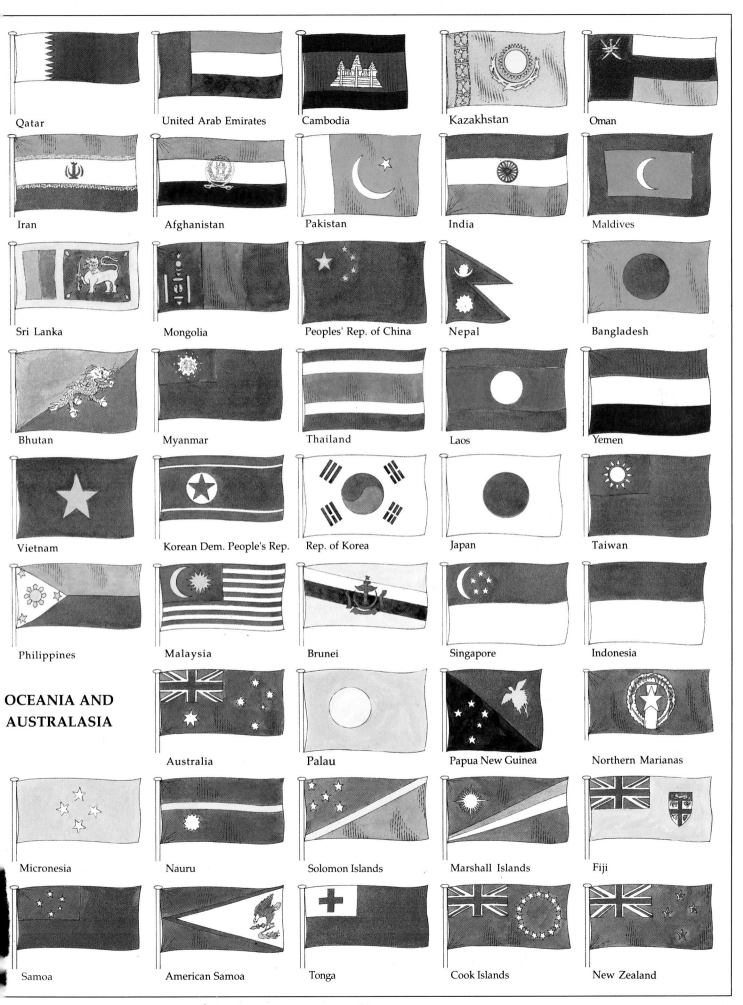

Qatar

United Arab Emirates

Cambodia

Kazakhstan

Oman

Iran

Afghanistan

Pakistan

India

Maldives

Sri Lanka

Mongolia

Peoples' Rep. of China

Nepal

Bangladesh

Bhutan

Myanmar

Thailand

Laos

Yemen

Vietnam

Korean Dem. People's Rep.

Rep. of Korea

Japan

Taiwan

Philippines

Malaysia

Brunei

Singapore

Indonesia

OCEANIA AND AUSTRALASIA

Australia

Palau

Papua New Guinea

Northern Marianas

Micronesia

Nauru

Solomon Islands

Marshall Islands

Fiji

Samoa

American Samoa

Tonga

Cook Islands

New Zealand

Index

Acknowledgments

Dorling Kindersley would like to thank:
For providing flags and other artefacts for photography:
Barbara Tomlinson, David Spence, Jim Stephenson, and the staff of the National Maritime Museum; Sylvia Hopkins and the staff of the National Army Museum; Sybil Burnaby and the staff of the Heralds' Museum; the College of Arms; the Royal Hospital of Saint Bartholomew; River Mill Flags; Turtle and Pearce Ltd; Black and Edgington Flags; Newitt and Co; John Eagle; the Flag Institute.
J. P. Brooke-Little and R. C.

Yorke for information on heraldry. Ray Allen of the Imperial War Museum for information and photographs. Vicky Davenport for advice on the planning of the book. Miranda Kennedy and Richard Czapnik for design assistance. Meryl Silbert. Fred Ford of Radius Graphics for paste-up

Photographers Karl Shone, Martin Plomer
Illustrators John Woodcock, Will Giles
Picture research Stasz Gnych, Angela Murphy

Picture credits
t=top b=bottom m=middle l=left r=right

Bibliotheque Nationale, Paris: 10 br
Bridgeman Art Library: 16tl, 17mr, 18m, 19bl, 26t, 26ml, 26br, 36ml, 46tr, 46mr, 49bl, 52tr, 54tr
British Museum: 8tl, 12cl, 36tr
Camera Press: 18br, 21m, 21br, 25bl, 28tl, 32mr, 32bm, 32br, 33bl, 38m, 38bl
College of Arms: 10mr, 11tl, 18tl
Colorsport: 20tl, 20 tr, 20br, 54b
Mary Evans Picture Library: 7tl, 7tr, 9tl, 13c, 14m, 22tl, 22mr, 24tl, 30ml, 30mr, 32bl, 36bl, 36br, 39bl, 44ml, 46bl, 47bl, 50tl, 56tl, 56ml, 54m, 55bl, 58br
GAMMA: 37br
Susan Griggs Agency: 34br, 35mr
Michael Holford: 8bl, 12tl

Robert Hunt: 13mr, 13tl, 17bl, 19m, 23tr, 24tr, 24m, 28br, 29bl, 34ml, 46mr, 52br, 57mr, 57bl
Imperial War Museum: 13br, 24mr, 28bl, 29br, 30tl, 47br, 55br
Popperfoto: 6tr, 42bl
Rex Features/SIPA Press: 19tl, 41bm, 44tr, 47ml, 51bl, 53mr, 57ml, 59br
Science Photo Library/NASA: 25br
Frank Spooner Pictures: 18ml, 24br, 30br, 31b, 50br
TRH/Tass: 23m
US National Archives: 25m